Representations

Student Research
in Visual Sociology and
the Sociology of Story

Edited by Naomi Alsop, Steve Birks,
Marc Bush, Lee Pinfold and
Emma Vryenhoef

The Reinvention Centre
For Undergraduate Research

The Reinvention Centre for Undergraduate Research

Department of Sociology

University of Warwick

Coventry

CV4 7AL

Email: reinvention@warwick.ac.uk

www.warwick.ac.uk/go/reinvention

The Reinvention Centre for Undergraduate Research, 2006

Series Editors: Hannah Bradby and Cath Lambert

Printing and cover design by Etrinsic: Stratford Road, Shirley, West Midlands, B90 4AD

Front cover image: *Coventry University's Lancaster Library (two-tone)* by Emma Vryenhoef

Back cover image: *Faces (two-tone)* by Steve Birks

ISBN-10: 0-9554207-0-9

ISBN-13: 978-0-9554207-0-2

A catalogue record for this book is available from the British Library.

Acknowledgements

We would like to acknowledge the work of all those who contributed to the book. Their research has inspired us and hopefully we have done it justice. Many others influenced the final outcome of this project. In particular we would like to thank Cath Lambert and Adam Cartwright at the Reinvention Centre for Undergraduate Research for their patience, support and encouragement. Many thanks go to Hannah Bradby for her faith in our work and for inspiring us to share it in the form of this book. Thank you to Carol Wolkowitz and Phil Mizen for their innovative and challenging module. We would also like to thank Louise Gregory, Sam Platts, Arran O'Kane, Pippa Daikin and Adele Ferrarin for their time and enthusiasm. To Dan Birks for assistance in the technical production of this book, your patience has been invaluable.

Contents

Book 1: The Sociology of Story

Part 1: Disease

Part 2: Death

Part 3: Difference

Part 4: Reflections on learning

Book 2: Visual Sociology

Part 1: Picturing the Social World

Part 2: Reflections on Learning

Foreword: A Story of Reinvention

Representations: Student research in Visual Sociology and the Sociology of Story is many things. It is a book of stories and pictures. It represents a creative and intellectual engagement with sociological questions. It is a teaching and learning resource, telling and showing us something about the experiences of doing sociology in different ways. It is also, perhaps most importantly, a book which has been conceptualised, written and produced by undergraduate students.

Students are producers of real knowledge. Whilst few of us in Higher Education might seek to actively deny this, university curricula, pedagogies and methods of assessment sometimes fail to recognise students' creative potential to establish research problems, to engage in research activities and represent their ideas in meaningful and intellectually challenging ways. In contrast, *Representations* not only entertains and educates the reader through image and story, but demonstrates the active and critical ways in which students can participate and intervene in the design and delivery of teaching and learning. By presenting their own experiences of learning through the sociology of story and image, *Representations* serves as a resource for other students and educators which, the contributors hope, will inspire similar student-led ventures in other, perhaps as yet unimaginable, shapes and forms.

A commitment to encouraging undergraduate students to contribute to the research culture of their departments is one of the core principles of the Reinvention Centre for Undergraduate Research. The Reinvention Centre is a collaborative Centre for Excellence in Teaching and Learning based in the Department of Sociology at Warwick and the School of the Built Environment at Oxford Brookes. For those of us based in the Reinvention Centre at Warwick, it has been pleasure and a privilege to witness the development of *Representations* from idea to publication, and to see, once again, that with appropriate academic and financial support, students educate and amaze with what they produce.

Although *Representations* represents the culmination of one aspect of this collaborative venture, it is only the beginning of the story. The images and narratives contained within its pages are now 'out there', taking on lives of their own as they are viewed, read, analysed and experienced. For the student editors, their hope is that they have illustrated and written the opening chapter of a new pedagogic story, and that the subsequent pages will be filled by, and with, other students and educators who are interested, inspired and challenged by *Representations*. I look forward to where the story takes us next.

Cath Lambert

The Reinvention Centre for Undergraduate Research

Editors' Introduction

During the academic year 2005-2006, two complementary developments in the Department of Sociology at Warwick provided the impetus for this edited collection. The first was the introduction of two new undergraduate modules: *Visual Sociology* and *Narratives of Death, Disease and Difference: the Sociology of Story*. The second was the work of the Reinvention Centre for Undergraduate Research. Whilst the Reinvention Centre emphasised the importance of undergraduate students doing research and contributing to the research culture of their department, *Visual Sociology* and *The Sociology of Story* gave us the opportunity to explore complex debates around production and interpretation of qualitative data in the form of pictures and text. *The Sociology of Story* introduced us to using fiction and biography in our research and writing, while *Visual Sociology* introduced us to photography as data. The process of adapting to and experimenting with these new methodologies was initially disconcerting but through the course of the year we acquired new skills. The two modules provided us with different ways of engaging with theory, encouraging us to think critically about our work through research-based learning.

During the course of the modules, and in the production of the book, we also found that we developed a greater level of reflexivity about our research and writing which we were able to apply to other areas of sociology. When we sat at the keyboard or looked through the camera lens we grew in our understanding of the power relations between the sociologist and those he or she hopes to represent; a recurrent theme in *Visual Sociology* was the power of the photographer over the photographed. We were encouraged to think about the process of making (rather than taking) pictures. Photographs have often been seen as an infallible form of evidence, but we quickly learned to appreciate how photography is often imbued with the photographer's intensions. Similarly, in *The Sociology of Story* we were encouraged to think about the image that we, as sociologists and writers, painted for the reader and to be deliberate about the effect that we intended.

As editors we have appreciated the opportunity to see other perspectives on the work we have undertaken and the range of approaches on to the topics we have studied through reading other students' submissions. We have been grateful for the opportunity to share the research in this book with a wider audience and we hope it gives some insight into the experiences of students as researchers, as well as showing that undergraduate students can be producers as well as consumers of knowledge. We hope that *Representations* is a step towards undergraduate student led research, publication and innovation at Warwick and beyond.

Naomi Alsop, Steve Birks, Emma Vryenhoef, Marc Bush and Lee Pinfold

Sociology of Story

Making a new module: Narratives of disease, death and difference: the sociology of story

Hannah Bradby
Module Convenor

Like many other sociologists of illness, I was struck by the number and popularity of published accounts of people's experience of serious illness during the 1990s. Oscar Moore wrote about living with HIV up to the time that he died of an AIDS-related illness. Ruth Picardie's columns in the Observer, written while she received treatment for cancer, made reference to John Diamond's stories of his treatment, appearing in The Times. Like Moore, Picardie and Diamond both died and had their columns published in book form. The popularity of these books seemed to mark the end of a reluctance to discuss serious disease in public and perhaps the beginning of a fascination with first person reporting from the cancer clinic. An online science and technology writer for the BBC, Ivan Noble documented his experience of a malignant brain tumour in a diary written for the BBC website. His worries, reflections, hopes and joys were documented, including his acknowledgement of his imminent death in a final diary entry that appeared a few days before he died. Death is often treated as a very private business, in which only close family have guaranteed rights to participate. So what does it mean to share one's death with thousands of readers? Like Moore, Picardie and Diamond, Noble was a journalist and his columns, like theirs, were snappy, witty pieces about suffering, treatment and the changes to identity wreaked by illness. Picardie, Moore and Noble were in their thirties when they died, while Diamond, Noble and Picardie had young children which only added to the compelling nature of their stories.

The cultural shift in the popularity of writing about a personal experience of disease that turns out to be terminal is evident, not only in published books and online diaries, but also in the large number of blogs by people with diagnosed diseases and online memorials to people who have died. The proliferation of individual stories about disease and their role as entertainment or 'info-tainment' was one impetus to establish a new undergraduate module.

As well as being remarkable for their proliferation, first person accounts of illness and treatment often eloquently illustrate major sociological themes. For instance Picardie, Moore, Diamond and Noble's accounts describe the biographical disruption incurred by diagnosis, the difficulties of the doctor-patient relationship and the medical discussion of disease compared with their embodied experience of illness. I wanted to teach a module in which journalism, memoir and fiction were treated as forms of evidence to illuminate the sociological investigation of death and disease alongside more traditionally academic forms of writing. I wanted to investigate why ill people feel compelled to write their stories and why some of us need to read them. This involved thinking about the role of stories in society. What are stories for? Who tells them and why? Does a story-teller need an audience? What are the effects of writing stories, especially around disease and dying? The outline of the module that arose from these questions is reproduced below, with a couple of key texts.

The discussions, thinking and writing exercises that we undertook in class based on a wide range of texts generated some interesting answers to these questions. We thought about stories as the main way in which humans make sense of their lives and the particular need for them in times of trouble and suffering. Disease disrupts a taken-for-granted future and stories rebuild the link from a person's past without illness, through the current suffering, to another future. Stories are not the same as narratives, because they are crafted and constructed rather than continuous. Unlike daily life, stories need a beginning, a middle and an end. Whether documentary or fiction, to grip the reader's attention, a story needs to describe a problem that is addressed, resolved or otherwise transformed by the end of story.

How to assess a module that takes stories seriously as sociological evidence? Students' understanding of the sociology of story needed to be demonstrated with writing that drew on appropriate substantive material and explored the structure and effects of stories. The obvious means of doing this was through writing a story. Students expressed some uncertainty about undertaking assessed work in a genre that many had last encountered at primary school, but with encouragement the story-writing began. The best of the students' work were highly eloquent expositions of the themes of the module which also told a gripping and well-structured story; the great majority were original and serious attempts to get to grips with complex material, as you can see from the examples reproduced in this book.

One of the most rewarding aspects of this teaching was working with students on their writing and seeing how much it changed over the course of a twenty-week module. The first draft of most of the stories was stilted, halting and uncertain. One-to-one and small group discussion about what the story was trying to achieve and ways to produce the desired effect in terms of style and structure were translated into re-drafts that were greatly altered. Re-writing stories in response to my feedback and to peer-review from other students in the class was, for some students, very painful. But since the process of peer-review is integral to becoming a professional and a published writer, whether of academic texts, fiction or journalism, this part of learning to write is unavoidable.

Teaching doesn't necessarily work in the ways that a teacher plans or a student anticipates. Nonetheless, I hope that some of the insight into the process, discipline and excitement of writing stories that was generated during this class will stay with students and continue to inspire their writing.

Module Outline

Disease and death threaten the continuity and coherence of existence and disrupt the routinely told, normalised narratives of identity: feeling different from others in society as a result of experiencing illness is part of suffering. This module considers how stories about death, disease and difference describe and evaluate difficulties experienced by individuals and groups. Features of the way that stories are told are analysed using concepts from literary criticism and cultural studies. The structure and function of narratives from memoir, fiction, autobiography and ethnography are examined.

The roles and effects of story telling in re-constituting a legitimate self in the face of difficulty and disruption, especially the prospect of death and disease, are covered in the first half of the module. The ways that stories re-cast experience to resist dominant ideologies and represent a medical and social reality from the point of view of those marginalised from institutional power are considered. The second half of the module extends these ideas with consideration of writing about cultural and ethnic difference in different genres. Parallels between the remedial and therapeutic effects of making, re-making and asserting narratives in medical settings and the political resistance of story-telling are drawn. The claims of objective and subjective truth-telling of different types of writing are compared.

Key texts

Arthur Frank (1995) *The wounded storyteller: body, illness and ethics*. Chicago: Chicago University Press.

Richard Kearney (2002) *On stories*. (Series: Thinking in action). London: Routledge.

Illness stories

John Diamond (1998) *C: because cowards get cancer too*. London: Vermillion.

Oscar Moore (1996) *PWA: Looking AIDS in the face*. London: Picador.

Ivan Noble (2005) *Like A Hole In The Head: Living With A Brain Tumour*. London: Hodder.

Ruth Picardie (1998) *Before I Say Goodbye*. London: Penguin.

Part One: Disease

Kolkata Red

Natalia Shpakovata

Durga is the Goddess of deliverance, strong and brave, standing on a lion, holding up the head of a dead demon-man. In Sanskrit, Durga means a woman who is incomprehensible and difficult to reach. She is the Mother of the Universe, beautiful and terrifying, the female power of the world. Every year Bengalis celebrate this destroyer of demons during Durga Puja. It is celebrated by all, big and small and men, who just the night before painted their wives', daughters' and courtesans' faces shades of red, sometimes with shame, sometimes with blood, offer flowers and praise the Goddess.

Some people say she can be seen on the streets of Kolkata, wandering in a torn red saree, a baby in her hands. Some say the child cries, others that it is long dead and she carries around a rotting little corpse. People say different things. Neighbours whisper that she drowned herself that very night. Some claim she sold herself in the street until the end, or her father shot her. I pray she found light. I pray for forgiveness.

*   *   *

- The Goddess has blessed that girl. Such a good offer, *didi*! You are very lucky, with your situation, you know. And a good family like that! I told you, didn't I, after the way you celebrated *Durga Puja* this year, luck could not pass your home!

Durga tried not to breathe too loudly in her excitement, standing behind the curtain separating the dark, damp-smelling parlour from the wide veranda of her parents' Kolkata mansion. It is up to her now! If she is pretty enough and the boy takes a liking to her, *Baba* will not have to pay any dowry! Poor *Baba*. His family used to be one of the richest in the whole of Bengal but the feuds between brothers led to their ruin. He still had the mansion and the pride, one as mouldy as the other, and here she lived for what seemed like eternity, protected from reality and the indecent looks of street boys. She smiled. She knew she was beautiful and that it was her only hope. Ma's efforts with the turmeric and lentil flour baths and sandalwood face masks will not be wasted. She will be married! She tiptoed, smiling, to her room and switched on an ancient TV. StarMovies was playing the good old *DDLJ* and she imagined, in the sticky-thick, jasmine and *ghee* smelling air of a Bengali summer afternoon, the life ahead of her, filled with love at least as great as in the movies.

*   *   *

When Durga woke up, it was already dark and the room was filled with the smell of frying vegetables from downstairs. She looked around and almost laughed. Here, here, freedom is almost here! She loved her parents and they were always kind to her, but being the only child and always overly protected, she yearned for a different life – she wanted to wear glamorous clothes, go to restaurants, shop, be in love… She quickly changed her damp *salwar kameez* for a clean starched yellow *saree* and ran downstairs to meet her father at the door.

- Come, Durga, I have to speak to you – were his first words as he saw her.

- Yes, Baba.

- On Saturday people will come… a very great family! And a good boy, he is a doctor in London, very educated. You always knew I can't give dowry… but they agree anyway, just want the boy to see you before, whether you are as fair as in the picture and all. Ok? Are you happy? He is a good boy… are you happy?

-Yes, *Baba*!

And so she was, early on Saturday morning, lying in bed with her face covered in cucumber slices soaked in rose water (just one of many of ma's lifetime collection of fairness recipes). Without moving her head she stretched her arm and felt it again. So lovely! Ma brought it in last night just as she stood, depressed, in front of her wardrobe full of old printed *salwars* and some plain cotton *sarees*. It was silk. It was red and ivory, gently embroidered with gold on the borders and *pallu*. It was almost like a movie heroine costume! Durga removed the cucumber slices and dutifully wiped her face with cold milk left on her bedside table by her mother. The *saree* sparkled in the morning sun coming through the window and its 5 meters seemed like an easy road to love.

Soon Ma came to take her downstairs and smiled approvingly. Durga was a pretty girl, fair and glowing, with soft brown eyes, now lined with kohl almost as much as the Goddess's, and long black hair. Her figure, too, was perfect for her role as a housewife and a mother – not too thin, not too large. The ivory silk of the *saree* made her hair shine and the red and gold borders, traditional *puja* style, matched the blush on her cheeks. Ma fastened Durga's best gold chain around her neck, pulled the *pallu* over her head and led her to the veranda.

- Here she is, Pradip-*babu*, our doll – she heard her father's voice.

- Vah, vah, beautiful, like a rose, is she not, Bishu? – Father in law?

Durga lifted her eyes just a bit. Around the cane table laden full of delicious milk sweets and ghee-fried savouries sat her *baba*, nervous and proud, a man of his age, large and happy, a silent pale woman wearing as big gold chains as in any movie (her mother in law!) and He. Their eyes met and she lowered hers and knew she loved him – her husband, her God and protector for life. She did not look at him anymore and did not question her parents' choice. He was perfect.

*   *   *

From then on it was all a haze. Wedding preparations had to be fast for Biswajit to have time for a honeymoon before going back to England. She remembered how Ma cried the night after the engagement, folding the same red-bordered *saree*.

- Abroad they don't have *sarees* like this. It's the red dye. My poor child, how will you live there? It is the brightest in Kolkata. It's so cold there… Remember this colour – it is the colour of this city but also the colour of a woman, of her honour, of her luck. As long as you wear the mark of your husband's blood on your forehead, you are the Goddess.

She wore the same blood red colour at her wedding, only this time the *saree* was an even fancier gold thread embellished *Banarasi*. She liked to think it was no worse than Aishwarya's in *Devdas*. She walked the sacred steps around the fire in a dream and her life was complete when He smeared the red powder on her forehead. A wife!

*   *   *

Durga sat on the bed, arranged there carefully by the girls – her *saree's* folds perfect, her jewellery gleaming, *pallu* low over her face, flowers all around her. She breathed hard, expecting him, looking like a prince, to come in any moment and then, like the times in movies when her heart fluttered in uncertain expectation of the future, he will lift his bride's face, look at her for a long time and know he loves her; then he will hold her hands and ask her about herself, her dreams, hopes, tell her about his and they will sit the whole night making plans for the life ahead of them… He did come. He hugged her awkwardly and fell asleep. She felt almost disappointed that he was not one of those husbands married women used to whisper about over *shingaras* and *chai* gathered on someone's veranda, the men who 'did that' to their new brides on the very first night. She stared at him until the morning, promising herself that for the sake of love, she will take no notice of trivial pains.

The wedding was followed by a brief honeymoon in her new brother in law's bungalow near Cape Town. There were no sightseeing trips, no dancing in pretty *sarees* on mountaintops, no playing in the sea. But Biswajit was good to her and she learned to appreciate the smaller things in a remarkably short time. Her most treasured memory of the honeymoon became the day when he took her and his nephews to the park and bought them ice cream. There was a bit on her chin and he kissed it off.

On the last day, however, when peeling onions for lunch dishes with her sister in law, she suddenly felt the heat, the stuffiness of a tiny kitchen, the heavy smell of *ghee*, spices and onion overpowered her and she collapsed into the tray of cut up vegetables. She woke up in the car, with her sister in law chattering excitedly about how Durga must be pregnant, what a good wife, hopefully it is a boy! In the public hospital, they examined her and took a blood sample and declared she was not. It was then that she thought of children for the first time. Yes, she wanted them! Someone to belong to her completely, to care for with all her heart, someone who will never reject her care and love, someone to protect… yes, yes, children could bring so much happiness to her life! From then on she felt bitter disappointment every time she bled and tried not to think about that tiny hope that if she gives birth to a healthy boy, Bishu might love her just a little bit more…

*   *   *

Durga was scared of meeting her in laws again. They flew back after the wedding and she never even had a proper look at them. Her father in law's voice seemed nice. She was not sure about her mother in law though. Would she be the kindly second Ma like in *Roja* or hate her like in *Devdas*, she wondered as the plane started descending over Heathrow.

She was neither. Kanika was a woman of what back in Kolkata they called 'old school' – you could never know what she thought, how she felt, or who she was, except that she was a perfect wife. Respectably stout, always wrapped in a starched stiff cotton *saree* with wide borders, with a large red *bindi*, her lips never smiling except in a formal greeting to her husband's friends, her eyes never crying, her hands never stopping. She lived as a good wife should – her world revolved around her home, she cooked amazing delicacies smothered in *ghee* and went to temple twice weekly. She received Durga with one of her formal smiles and made sure the girl was kept at a reasonable distance. She prohibited nothing, but somehow, almost without words, made it clear that there will be no jeans and that the *pallu* should be drawn over the head in the presence of elders and strange men, that experiments with Italian recipes should not be a substitute for 6-curry meals and that good new daughters in law do not talk too much. This was just as well, for Durga rarely had someone to talk to – Bishu worked till late and liked to relax in front of a cricket match on TV with a plate of fresh *rosogollas* rather than sit with her in the bedroom, even though she wore a pretty *saree* and put her hair up every night; her mother in law was always busy, her father in law did not seem interested in anyone at home and spent most of his time in a café near the temple remembering old Kolkata with some other sad old men.

So days rolled by and Durga got used to her life. It was average. It was the same as lives of many young wives she met while distributing *prashad* at the temple or shopping in Southhall. Durga never complained, but could not help thinking about Rani often. Rani… she was Durga in her dream life. She came to temple every Friday with her husband, always in a new fancy *saree*, made to order copies of those in *Devdas, Hum Apke Hai Koun, Pareenita*… She always wore make up and smoked long white cigarettes in the car park. Her husband adored her   they always held hands and could not stop touching each other. Sometimes Durga thought that it was because they lived alone, no in laws, no distractions, just them… But sometimes she realized that it was because they loved each other and she and Biswajit did not. She pushed the thought to the back of her mind as fast as she could and hoped that tonight he will notice her efforts. She kept trying, sometimes only because she believed that she will only conceive a baby when he makes love to her passionately, lovingly, looking into her eyes, not like usually – once a week on a Saturday night, when he was least tired but slow from all the food, in the darkness, without kisses. Sometimes she wondered whether he was thinking about those thin blond girls in short skirts he stared after in the street.

*   *   *

- Shouldn't you see a doctor? – Durga's mother in law asked one morning.

- Why, Ma?

- You did not get your period this month. Maybe you are finally pregnant.

- How?..

How did the woman always know things? Surely she never even spoke to her mother in law about her periods. In any case, she was right and next day Durga went to see doctor Rai, a Bengali GP the family has been going to for years. He was all smiles.

- Congratulations, congratulations, pass my greetings to Bishu and your respected in laws! You are pregnant! We will just take some blood samples to check whether everything is fine so come again after a week and we can talk more.

A few days later the ceremony was held to bless the pregnant woman and her child. A priest was invited to pray for the successful birth of a son. Durga thought her mother in law's smile was almost genuinely happy and that night Bishu kissed her on the lips while making love. She felt a tingle of disappointment that all she could think about while he did it was her lovely new *saree* and a beautiful gold set her in laws gave her that day. She felt she got what she wanted from her husband and will never ever again be hurt by his indifference.

*   *   *

Almost a week later, when Durga was just sprinkling the mustard seeds into hot *ghee* for the fish curry, the phone rang and Dr Rai, in a strangely distant voice, asked her to come and see him as soon as possible. Her legs went numb and she could barely conceal her panic from her mother in law. What is wrong? He must have had the tests back and something must be wrong with her baby. But she did not feel unwell... how can it be? Will her baby die? Is it dead already? Why, why, why, God, please, no…

Somehow she carried on the whole afternoon, chopping and frying, dusting and lighting incense in the *puja* room, smiling while serving *chai* to her father in law. It was almost five when she finally managed to get out of the house and she ran all the way to Dr Rai's office. Durga was never this scared before, not on her wedding night, not when *Baba* had a stroke, not even when communal riots broke out in Kolkata and, hidden behind a curtain, she saw their neighbours' son cut the throat of his Muslim friend in his backyard. In the last few days she fell in love with the person inside her, fell in love with all the passion and intensity she once expected from a marriage. This new love she did not compare to anything she saw in the movies, it was too deeply part of her own being, something incomprehensible and holy. She felt like she carried the whole universe in her belly, a little sun-god that will make her life beautiful…

The meeting with Dr Rai was brief. It could not have lasted longer than 5 minutes. But it ended her life. Now the sun-god inside her was facing a demon, something dark and scary, a demon no one had managed to kill yet, a demon that she knew little about, except that he took away a lot of little gods with shiny black faces and tearful eyes.

*   *   *

Durga rolled into a ball under the blanket and waited for the phone to ring. She knew Dr Rai would call. She saw the disgust in his eyes. How could she explain that she never even looked at a man other than Bishu with any feeling? Everyone knew prostitutes, dancers, had these diseases. In her secluded life revolving around the old Kolkata mansion and a shady jasmine garden she learned little about death, but had heard about AIDS – she saw it on TV and once she heard aunty Geeta whisper to her mother that the Guptas' son really died of that – picked up from some whore, you know. Bad women have this. But how, how? She could only think of the honeymoon, the blood test. Did she see them taking out a new syringe? Did she? Did she? This does not happen to middle class Kolkata girls married to nice doctor boys from good Bengali families. This happens to street girls, girls who run away with Musulmans or white men, not her, not her, not her! Sometimes a person is long dead before their heart stops beating and Durga was already dead then. She did not think of treatment, she could only think of shame. Shame, shame, how will her parents ever look at people again?

After what seemed like hours of fear, Durga fell into heavy sleep and did not hear the phone ring, did not hear the silence that descended on the house as the family whispered in the kitchen, did not hear her father in law leave and her mother in law crying hysterically in the bathroom. She woke up when the door banged, finding the room dark and feeling guilty she is not in the kitchen grinding fresh garam masala or cutting up the bitter gourds. But it must have been night already. She tensed up. Did he know?

But Biswajit took his clothes off, put on his pyjamas and quickly fell asleep beside her. The house was quiet. No light came from her in laws' room. Did they know? What are they going to do to her? She shivered remembering stories of young wives whose *sarees* caught fire from stoves and lamps and whose parents never found justice for their murdered daughters. No, that is ridiculous. But they will hate her. Now he will never love her, never. Now her sun-god will die. They will throw her out, yes, surely. They will not keep a woman who will become known as a whore in their house. She must go. She must go home, back to the sun, to the warmth of Kolkata that cures all the pains with its almost poetic dirtiness, so horrible and divine at the same time, Bengal, Bengal... yes, home.

Money, she must find money. She will not take theirs. She has her own. Durga pulled out her large black suitcase from the back of the wardrobe and found the envelope under piles of *sarees* and shawls. Oh, the eternal wisdom of Mothers! Ma collected this money for decades, bits saved on groceries, gifts... she gave it to Durga the night before she left Kolkata.

- Sometimes a woman needs something of her own. It is not much but keep it, my darling. If you never need it, use it to buy your own daughter a beautiful golden bangle. Keep it.

Now she needed it, just enough for a ticket. Durga did not take any jewellery. Let them have it as the dowry they so graciously did not take, a compensation for a bad daughter in law. She left as she was, in a creased red cotton *saree* with dark green borders, her hair still shiny with coconut oil she applied in the morning, taking just her handbag, the money, a packet of spicy puffed rice from the kitchen, the god and the demon inside her. On the plane she wrapped her *saree* around her, hugged her only slightly rounding belly and dreamt of her mother, her soft, soft arms, *paan*-stained smile, red-bordered cotton *sarees*, neat line of *sindoor* on the parting of grey hair. She was herself still a child and believed that somewhere in Kolkata, in the old mansion, in her mother's magic box filled with herbs, fairness mixtures, recipe cut-outs, old *bindis* and half-used pots of Tiger balm, there will be a remedy even for AIDS, even for ignorance.

*   *   *

We called her parents when we discovered she was gone in the morning. We told them they gave us a used woman, a loose woman, shame on them. They said nothing, shamed. When she came home, half conscious with hunger and tiredness, she found the gate locked and all the windows shut. She knocked for a long time, she cried and begged. The gate never opened. She left eventually, in the darkness of the same sweet Bengali night filled with music and prayers of *Durga puja* as the one when she tried on her wedding *saree*. Did she die that night or did she find out that a few days later her *Baba* shot himself with his father's partition-time gun, leaving her Ma at the mercy of judging relatives, who whispered about mothers who bring up whores until she followed her husband to the next incarnation?

*   *   *

I came back to Kolkata a year after she left, during *Durga puja*. I came to see my relatives or maybe to look for her. But where do you look for an ill 20 year old girl in the streets of Kolkata? There are thousands of them, beautiful flowers that grew in the wrong gardens and I turn and look for a long time at torn red *sarees* along the streets. Some of them beg from the passing cars, some sell biscuits and coconuts, some – themselves, and some are just dying. Who are they? Someone's daughters, wives, sisters… daughters in law of stupid old men like me… unprotected, unloved, blamed. Some of them still wear *sindoor* on the partings of dirty greying hair, a tribute to demon-gods who betray them, same red powder we worship the Goddess with. Shame. Shame…

GLOSSARY

Aishwarya – Aishwarya Rai, popular Bollywood actress.

Baba – father (Bengali).

Babu – respectable form of address, sir.

Banarasi – a type of saree, embroidered with gold and usually worn by brides.

Bindi – a dot of sindoor on a woman's forehead.

Chai – traditional tea prepared with milk, sugar and spices.

DDLJ – common abbreviation for Dilwale Dulhania Le Jaenge (*The one with the pure heart will get the bride*) – one of the most popular Bollywood films of all time, starring Shah Rukh Khan and Kajol.

Didi – elder sister, a respectful form of address.

Ghee – clarified butter.

Oi – it is bad luck for a Bengali Hindu wife to address her husband by his name, so calls like Oi and hey are common.

Paan – betel leaf filled with spices and specialist mixtures traditionally chewed by Bengalis, especially women, who can not smoke due to the social stigma. Prolonged use stains teeth with red.

Pallu – the most elaborate end of a saree which is draped over the shoulder, displayed on the arm or used as a veil.

Prashad – 'blessed food' distributed freely after pujas in many Hindu temples.

Puja – worship, prayer, religious celebration.

Rosogolla – traditional Bengali sweet balls made with cottage cheese and soaked in rose-scented syrup.

Salwar Kameez – loose tunic worn over wide trousers and combined with a large scarf (dupatta) usually hung to hide the breasts.

Shingara – fried Bengali pastry with spicy potato filling.

Choices

Steve Birks

'Why? O, why? O, why?' escapes from Mark's lips before he can silence himself and return to his worrying, about worrying, about being worried, about deciding things.

He makes such a big issue of the trivia of the day; even where to park his car is a major issue for him. He takes thirty minutes to drive to work and spends all of this thinking time debating with himself where to park and which way to walk from the car park to the office. Should he take the short walk this morning, through the car park, along the road, down the alley and save the longer walk to pay for his parking this evening.... or should he do it the other way around? He occasionally can't help exclaiming out loud to himself. It's his way of confirming his decisions when he finally manages to make them.

'The long way.........'

Some say it's the first sign of madness.

And he worries about this.

He reassures himself by making one final check of the change in his pocket, by running his fingers over the change in his pocket to be sure that he has the right change for the machine this evening in his pocket. A pound coin, a fifty and four tens...

'Exactly!' That is exactly what he needs. £1.90.

Day in day and day out on his few minutes walk from the car to the office, he passes people going purposefully on their way and he worries.......

'Do they worry?'

He wants to know if they have the same difficulty with the little things in life as he does? Do they get bothered about everyday choices? What choices do they have to make? How do they do it? Do they do it? Is it as hard for them as it is for him?

'Can I tell?'

He thinks he might find some answers to his worries in their faces. So this morning he looks at their faces rather closely. He usually avoided looking at their faces, as he may have to return their glance. From his careful

observations, Mark recorded this morning, one hello, two nods and one smile, not much to go on. In the background, almost unnoticed it's so regular, the endless, endless chak, chak, chak chatter of Magpies; he likes it and finds it quite reassuring.

There are many more of these crafty birds around than there used to be. They are being unreasonably blamed for the disappearance of songbirds from the countryside, parks and gardens.

He just wonders if these tuxedoed prophets really know the future.

'One's for sorrow! Two for joy,' He really needs to know how the rest goes. It's Monday, so he chooses the promise of sorrow. To him it seems appropriate as he loathes the first day of the week. Who doesn't?

He's like clockwork, collecting his post mechanically every day from the pigeonholes that cover half of reception's back wall. Receiving paper messages like shortwave radio from the darkest distances of the globe. And the pit that is admin. The holes classify and order the paper missives. A to Z, three compartments for the b's, two for a's. He frets and wonders if there are really mores b's than a's in the world or do b's just get more post and messages? He stops his world tour, returns to reality, becoming conscious that his pigeonhole is quite full this morning.

He slowly sorts through the letters; Brown, Brown, Box, Bliss, Bird, Brown, Brown, Brown, Brown, Brow........Linda; he just wishes she'd collect her post every day.

'She's never here!'

For the last year, her depressing tones have been ringing in his ears. He's heard her say in her negative drone a million times: 'I can't do that. It won't work. That's not possible!' and if all else fails, 'I have too much to do.....I can't!' He could go on, but his thoughts are cut short by Jo from upstairs.

'Hi, Mark. Ms B's not in today by the look of her post you've got there.'

'I guess not, Jo' Mark replies. 'She seems to be more part time than full time; I wish I could get away with taking so much time off.'

'Yea.' And as a parting shot Jo throws in, 'catch you later for coffee, if you ever get that lot sorted out'.

He neatens her post, the largest C4 to the left, next the C5s, then C6s and finally DLs, those without windows first, then those with windows, he likes and needs envelopes to be this way. He's fixated with order and he's even happier when he knows the pages inside are unfolded, A4 paper in C4 envelopes, A5 in the C5s. He hates A4 paper triple folded in DLs. He always uses C4 envelopes so that his letters are unfolded, the thought of his mail arriving crisp and unfolded gives him a rare sense of contentment. He sees them flat and crisp, resting in plastic in-trays. This desire for order preoccupies his day. First he tidies his desk, then his shelves, then spends the rest of his day in the stationery room trying to create some sort of satisfying order. Mark gets no real work done.

*   *   *

Where to park today? He has been wondering and he can't make up his mind. So he lets the weather make the choice for him today, it's easier. Surely even he can't be unaffected by the wonder that comes with this wind. It has the first sign of autumn under her wing – fresh – it carries a taste, as sharp as green apples. And with the chill, a warm frosting of new colour to the trees, a prelude to the performance that is autumn.

This fine morning brings Mark on his way from car park to desk; three hellos, two nods, and one smile; there is no great improvement because of the weather. As always, most people are reacting not to the best but to the worst, the chill in the air sends them scurrying and they miss the hidden beauty of the day.

And today there are three prophets chaking, 'One for sorrow! Two for joy! Three for a girl!'

From this omen, he expects Linda's post to be gone and for her to be at work.

'Those damn birds got it wrong!'

He is now in a stew, Ms. Brown!

He really doesn't want to have to sort your post, he thinks it's your job. You wouldn't expect him to empty your bin, or wash your coffee cups or answer your emails, but you expect him to move your post, day in day out, shuffle it into order, move it out of the way and put it back. You may not care, but he does.

'Maybe I should just chuck the lot in the bin!' he muttered under his breath.

At least it would be out of his way. But fortunately for him and office politics, he shows more common sense and just starts to return her letters to their proper place.

'Hi Mark, Linda's not in. Have you heard what's up with her .... again!'

'Naw Jo. It maybe the Monday Blues or Tuesday blues .... or just the blues.' He is preoccupied with his post and her post, but manages to show a little concern. 'She has seemed a bit more down than usual.'

Jo's now wound up, 'For God's sake we all feel down sometimes Mark. Up tight, stressed out, too much to do, but you just have to get on with things!'

'Yea! She just needs to pull herself together. Maybe she needs to be told to pull her weight. It's just not fair on the rest of us having to do her work.'

'So true Mark. But got a meeting so must go. See you later'

'See you!'

Jo's great contribution to office life is deftly adding fuel to any fire.

But Mark can't see; he's too preoccupied with his own worries about making day to day decisions. He can't see that Linda's life is not fine. Because she's at home, he imagines she's in bed, safe and warm just as his own bed is the best and safest place in the world to be.

On Saturdays and Sundays he never deserts his bed so that there are no choices to make. He thinks of it as resting his brain, chilling out. He believes it is what real people would do if they could. He does things the right way - it's the only way to be ordered and controlled. In his small dingy kitchen the cups are in a line, handles all pointing east, the cans and the jars are all in alphabetical order. He switches and unplugs all of his appliances at night; the central heating is timed to the hour and the second. Even though he then overrides the controls and then forgets and lets it runs to maximum 24 hours a day 365 days of the year, it's not something that bothers him.

What he can control is controlled to the accuracy of a millionth of a millimetre. He only lets the things into his life that he can control - they are the only things he lets matter - the rest are nothing. Total control of the few things that he lets matter, matter. It's only the things he lets matter that matter to him; his life then, he sees, is OK.

He lost control of his wife, his kids, his new wife, his new kids, his smart home, but at least the cup handles point east now. Therefore life's OK.

*   *   *

Across the town, Linda is planning her day.

She murmurs her well practiced morning litany.

'Just five more minutes.' 7:45 a.m.

And

'Just five more minutes.' 7:50 a.m.

And

'Just five more minutes.' 7:55 a.m.

And

'Just five more minutes.' 9:00 a.m.

She then slips into 21 minutes of fitful exhausting dreaming, half-awake half-asleep, sweaty - waking more tired than before. Eyes tight shut, clamped against the world. A million feathers cling to her; creating from her sweat and body heat, a warm damp womb.

She tells herself, 'I will - I will - I must,' but perhaps not today.

Every morning it's the same, she plays it over in her mind, she plans to go to work tomorrow, and tomorrow she will collect her post bright and early, write that report that's over due and be positive. She knows it's OK at work; she can function at work; she knows she can, it's the getting ..... started it's the .... start of the day, she just can't manage it.

'Just five more minutes.' 9:21 a.m. and 30 seconds.

9.25 a.m. her phone rings for the first time today. She leaves it, it will only be work or a call-centre.

9.35 am her phone rings for the second time today. She leaves it, it will only be work or a call-centre.

She finally summons up all of her strength and reaches the bathroom, but can't make the effort to clean her teeth – she tells herself no one will know. She splashes cold water on her face. Looking in the mirror, she can see in her face the long restless night just passed and she can see the long flat-battered day to come that is reflected in her eyes. Her favourite room on these days is the living room. It only has a north-facing window and with the heavy curtains drawn, it shuts out the day. Wrapped in her duvet she zaps TV stations, it makes her feel involved in life although she never watches a program for more than a few moments and if she does and any real life presents itself, she moves on. She has the weather forecast off to a fine art. Enjoying the World's weather the most, it's so distant and unreal it's nothing to do with her, the Scottish and Northern Irish weathers are also OK. Welsh weather's not too bad, but is getting close to home; the north of England is too close to home as she knows people who live there. All she has to do is flick the button when things get too close to home, but occasionally the effort's too great and she gets the start of the Midlands' forecast. If only pressing the button wasn't so hard, she'd never need to know what's outside.

Her phone rings for the umpteenth time today. She leaves it, as it will only be a call-centre; no one other than work or sales staff ever calls.

Why doesn't she unplug it? It would drive me mad! Then again maybe she is a little mad.

Her need for lunch arrives at four pm. Resisting her hunger requires greater effort than scraping some margarine on toast and making a soggy crisp sandwich from the half-eaten packet of cheese and onion crisps. She washes it down with tepid tea; to find the switch on the kettle is too much of an effort. She no longer tastes her food and drink, she even ignores the taste of gone off milk, her food just fills a physical gap.

The phone rings yet again, and again.

By late afternoon she collagging ....

'Look! I know it's not a word but I'm the narrator! It says the right things so it's staying put!'

.... the soaps that she has already seen once today on TV, but her difficulty comes with the wall to wall Evening News bringing reality into her living room. 'For God's sake,' she spits out and at the moment any old god will do, as she needs this to be a living room not a dying room. It makes her feel so bad that the reality of washing up is better than the reality of this misery. She washes up, her first activity of the day, then drags herself back to her duvet.

The phone rings yet again, and again, but this time as its after 9.30 p.m. it won't be work or any one selling anything so she summons up the energy to answer.

'Hi Mum, I've been trying to phone you for hours. I've been up all night trying.'

'Is that you really you dear? It's been so long.'

'Yes! Mum it's me.'

'I'm out of money, so I'll come home.'

'Oh, when?'

'As fast as you can send me some money for my ticket Mum. I'll pay you back.'

'That's OK dear, when you can.'

Linda was at the bank by five to nine the next day, first in the queue waiting for the doors to open.

For Mark, no question of where to park today, he can only abdicate the choice and takes the longest walk possible. Even he realises that only a fool would miss out on the glory that is today. Autumn's alchemy is in the world, dancing through every tree, fields of flowers against the sky.

The weather is working its magic on the souls around Mark; he counts six hellos, two nods, and six smiles. One for sorrow! Two for joy! Three for a girl! Four for a boy! Five for ! Six for !

There were two magpies on the path today.

One for sorrow! Two for joy!

'Hi, Linda!' He is relieved she's back at work at last.

'Thank God!' but ..... perhaps not .... he realises that after a few hours of her 'can't-ing' she will be just as irritating as ever.

'How are you Linda?'

'Hi, ya. Great thanks Mark.'

He inspects her closer, she is looking brighter, 'You're looking fresher.'

'Yeah I've just had a shower, I've done the gym, did lots of rep' and I've been for a run.'

She then offered to get Mark a drink!!!!!!!!!!!!

'Could I get you a cup of coffee or tea, latté, filter, milk sugar, de-caf, Fair Trade, tea with milk, without?' she offered Mark.

'That's not the order they are on the board Linda.'

'So live dangerously Mark,' is her tart reply.

She remembers this prick has always got up her nose.

'Thanks very much for the offer Linda, but I need to take some time on that.'

Mark hides himself in the safety of his mantra, 'Seven a secret not to be-told! Eight for ! Nine for ! And Ten it's the devil's own self.'

But it still takes ten months to find a sympathetic GP who is understanding of Mark's condition.

Mark was retired from work on medical grounds and now receives sickness benefit. It pays him just enough to live on. He can often be seen feeding his only friends, the Magpies, in the park near his flat and taking their chak, chak, chaking advice to help him shape his day. Some days are better for him than others and he seems to take some pleasure from the simple events of the day. On bright sunny days he smiles and nods to people and in the autumn he enjoys the simple pleasure of collecting and sorting coloured leaves. He arranges them in order, all the oranges together, all the yellows together and all the reds together. In his hand, he holds the largest to the left and on the right the smallest. Never more than ten at a time, as his feathered friends only count to ten, but at last, his days have some order and his devils are held at bay.

Ghosts

Laura Percival

Vince, I feel bad about everything *all* the time.

I was on the phone to Vince. I had met him at a concert and I think he saw something inside me. He certainly couldn't have seen much on the outside. I gave him my number, feeling stupid because I knew he would never call. Nobody ever did. I don't mean that in a self-pitying way, I just can't imagine why anybody would want to phone me when I don't ever phone them. Three weeks after the concert, the phone rang.

'Hey is that Allie? It's Vince. We met a few weeks ago, remember?'

Oh yes. Bliss!

I hadn't met Vince again. He was very busy. However, he always called me with lots of little pearls of wisdom. I appreciate it on some level.

'Hey Allie, don't feel bad. You put too much emphasis on little situations when you don't need to. Sometimes life needs to wash over you, like the sea. Know what I mean?'

Other levels wonder if he is mocking me, recording my miserable ramblings for his friends to listen to. Amusement at my expense. Why would anybody want to call up a woman they've only met once, just to hear her sob?

Linda tells me I am too paranoid, and need to work more on my trust issues. I tell Linda time again that I don't have paranoia, that people just don't like me. She says that everything will be OK in time. I just need to keep taking my pills and my brain will eventually find its balance. I don't take my pills. That's a secret that only Vince knows, as he is the only one I talk to now. I don't know what these pills do. What if they have some kind of **poison** in, to kill off the undesirables in society? What if they are a kind of biological tracking device? No way am I subjecting myself to that. They can't fool me.

You can't trust doctors or nurses these days, Vince once told me. He said that over half the pills they sell in the US are placebos, yet the economy is held stable by the pharmaceutical companies. It's people like me and you who they exploit as pawns in their little game. I said I didn't know if that was true, even though I usually agree with what he says. I said goodbye and hung up the phone.

I need to devise a plan for the day ahead. If I don't list things, then I can't function properly. Everything I do is in list form, on sticky notes. Prioritising soothes me.

Get Dressed.

Make Tea.

Should I compensate for being hungry? Sometimes I am ravenous, other times I don't eat all day. Linda chastises me for not having set meal times as part of my routine. She says meal times are the most important part of the day. I panic as I forget what else I have to do tomorrow. I decide, instead, to give myself some tasks, as Linda says keeping busy will help towards a speedy recovery.

Eat (or not).

Wash Dishes.

Paint Nails.

You should always aim to look nice and presentable. What if somebody came to the door? What if a relative should visit? I would feel terrible if I looked bad, and they might guess that something was wrong.

Linda at 11.00.

What else? Something might present itself tomorrow. You Never Can Tell.

Before I attempt to sleep, I have a bath. I must always have a bath, because throughout the day little impurities stick to your skin. As the air molecules rush past you, all the air-born bacteria cling on, in order to find some place that they might live, or **infect**. Other people's smoke and flakes of skin and diseases all float around in the air as well. These must all be washed off before I can sleep. I don't know whether I like water or not. It seeps into crevices and cuts, and I don't like the idea of being infiltrated by water, like a sponge. On the other hand, it is warm and I feel like nothing can hurt me once I am enclosed. I try not to think about water-born viruses and instead I close my eyes and imagine that I'm swimming in some tropical sea, with only beautiful fish and plants for company.

Then I go to bed, where I lie awake thinking about Everything, until I fall asleep but the Everything is still there. Only instead of just being Everything, it is a **muddle** of things and the Everything gets much worse.

Allie? Allie?

Somebody was shaking me. Where was I?

I could hear lots of noise in the background, but at the same time hear nothing. I couldn't move, my vision was blurred and a sharp pain flashed across my forehead. I didn't know where I was or what had happened. I couldn't even remember my name.

My old house was a mess. I shared it with two guys I met when I was working in a bar and they let me move in when I had nowhere else to go. We were like a little family. I lost my job and spent quite a while just looking after them. I would get up in the morning, make coffee and pour myself some, before taking it into Daniel's room, because he was usually awake at the same time as me. Then I would take it into the living room to where Rich had inevitably fallen asleep, so that the coffee would stay warm in the pot and would wake him up as the smell drifted around the room. We didn't have enough money to buy food, and the fridge didn't work. Instead, we filled it with foil and used ice packs and beer to keep it cold. The house had four rooms; two bedrooms, a bathroom, and a kitchen/diner/living room combination. The wallpaper was peeling off the walls because of the condensation and it was covered in strange burn marks, which were already there when I moved in. Daniel would go out with girls who worked in fast-food restaurants or supermarkets so he could get us food for free. Rich drank a lot, slept all day, and played his guitar all night. He thought he was going to be the Next Big Thing. It wasn't the way I'd planned on living my life, but it worked well and was fun. Life was a breeze.

Things began to change when, by chance, I got a job working in a carpet warehouse. The money was terrible, but it put food on the table. Rich spent a lot of the money on alcohol, and Daniel was hardly at home. I was feeling used and rejected.

Is she able to talk?

Miss – we need to talk to you.

Your friend...

I had a call from the carpet warehouse one morning. My boss, Mr. Naylor, had wanted to know if I planned on coming into work again. Since I had not renewed my sick leave, technically I was due into work. Yes, I said. I am very sorry and I shall be in tomorrow. Tomorrow never came.

In the morning, I wake up and look and think. I think for hours and then Do Things that make up the rest of the day. I tried to make Mr. Naylor understand, but he didn't want to know. He said I could either come to work, quit, or get fired. I think he fired me. Either way, I can't really remember and it was just after that when I met Vince. Daniel moved out of the house, he said he couldn't be there after Rich died, but I got the feeling he couldn't stand to put up with me any longer. I think maybe it was because I stopped making him coffee in the morning.

Your friend...

Is dead.

What?

WHAT?

When Rich had driven the car into the one coming in the opposite direction, I was only saved because of the way the car had spun. The driver's side had crumpled like paper. They asked me questions. Had we been drinking?

I couldn't remember. I couldn't even remember them telling me, a week after. I dreamt about it. I knew I had a bitch of a headache that had lasted for three weeks, but people came and went. They had no faces.

~~Get Up.~~

~~Get Dressed.~~

~~Make Tea.~~

~~Eat (or not).~~

What do I want to eat? Am I hungry? Is there any benefit in eating? I decide that yes, there is, because if I don't eat something then I get shaky and then I get clumsy and when I accidentally break something then I get angry and break something else on purpose and then I hurt myself and then I cry and then I hate myself. I feel like food sticks to the inside of my ribcage and instead of goodness being absorbed into my bloodstream, sugar and fat work their way inside instead. I choose an orange. Vitamin C helps to banish the multitude of toxins that soak through your skin during the day. Vince sometimes says that if I eat nothing else during the day, then I should eat fruit. Vince is usually right, so I follow his advice to the letter. I have no advice from anywhere else. You can't trust anybody.

~~Wash Dishes.~~

~~Paint Nails.~~

Linda at 11.00.

I don't really listen to Linda when she talks. I look at her. She has mousy brown hair, always pulled back and her eyes sag and look sad all the time. Her face annoys me. She speaks about the pills redressing the chemical balance in my brain and the importance of routine. She wants to know what I have done this week. Have I been out the house? Have I had any visitors? I tell her about Vince. She seems pleased that I have regular contact with somebody. She asks if I think the pills have been working. I tell her yes, I think so. Just behind Linda on the wall is a clock. I often look at clocks and panic because I think the small hand is going the wrong way.

What if time went backwards? Would we all get younger and forget all the things we know? It's OK because the hands are going the right way, but I know that if I keep staring, I'll think about all the things I was thinking about before and then - *Why the hell did you let him drive in that condition? Why did you get in the damn car Allie? Why? Why? Are you stupid? He's dead, Allie. Do you understand?*

I heard a noise like a high-pitched moan; I realised it was coming from me.

Speak to me! What the hell were you thinking?

Why Allie?

Linda was holding a shoebox, a shoebox that came from my bathroom. The one I had left on the floor the previous night after I had dropped it through being too shaky and gotten angry and thrown it. I sat and cried on the floor for so long that I couldn't bear to see it or touch it again and I had completely forgotten to put it away this morning.

'Why?'

I heard that high-pitched moan again. This time it was more of a pathetic squeak, rather than an expression of pain that had destroyed my soul.

'Why? Why haven't you been taking your pills?'

I didn't know why. The government didn't seem like the kind of excuse that would fool Linda.

I wasn't sure whether she was disappointed, like my mother was when she found out I hadn't been going to school, or angry, like Daniel was when he found out I'd let Rich drive.

Back, forwards, back, forwards

A buzzing

If this was a dream...

It would all go away.

*   *   *

In the hospital there are only two rooms that I use.

One is where my bed is and there are three other beds in the room. The first two days, I had the bed next to the door. I could hear banging and crashing and water running. When Jenny, the woman next to me in the window bed, left, I asked to be moved over.

Now I can see out of the window.

When I was young, my father worked away, and he used to say:

'At night, look up at the moon and know that I'll be looking at it too.'

Then he never came back. I knew he'd still be looking at the moon, wherever he was. The bastard.

I hope all the people I've ever run away from or upset sometimes look at the moon. I called Vince, for the first time ever and told him I was going away.

'Yeah.' chill out.' he said. 'Don't let them fool you, Allie. Keep aware.' And then I realised that it was His Fault I was in here.

He told me about the government and I don't even know him. He told me what to do. Nobody ever told me what to do. There are some things you can't write on a list and so I needed him to tell me.

He hasn't done anything wrong.

But

I am not afraid now.

I can make other friends. I've made them before.

The only other woman in my room now is called Anne and she wears a wig and thinks that government spy planes are following her and she checks under her bed every ten minutes for snipers. Sometimes she shouts 'Gas Attack!' and runs down the corridor with her hospital gown undone, flailing behind her.

I laughed for the first time since Rich died when that first happened.

The other room is the lounge. It has eight chairs, in a semi-circle around a television that is never on. If you have visitors, you can take them in there.

The chairs are big and soft, and made out of shiny green synthetic leather.

I used to have a leather skirt. I remember liking that leather skirt.

If I sat on these chairs in that skirt, the materials would rub together and squeak.

And that would be **funny**.

*   *   *

I was only there a week and one day. Janet, the ward manager, told me she was very pleased with me and that if I go home and continue my treatment, life should be **back to normal** in no time.

I moved in with my mother.

The only thing that annoys me is her choice of food. I'm very particular. She buys frozen fish instead of fresh, full fat instead of half fat and orange juice with bits in.

She comes into my bedroom every morning at 9am and says,

'Right, here is your drink and your pills: I've laid them out for you.'

And I take them. She watches. And then, she goes to my white cupboard, the same one I've had since I was born, and takes out an outfit for me to wear.

Jeans.

Baby blue shirt.

Black socks.

White underpants.

I like being told what to wear. I can say no if I want to.

She goes out the room whilst I dress and then comes with me to the living room, where the TV goes on and *Good Morning America* or some other such banal programme is playing. I sit down, and she makes me some breakfast. Today she brings it in on a tray: a pot of tea, with four slices of toast in the toast rack, full fat butter in a dish, and a small pot of jam. She eats with me and then we continue sitting for a while until we have something else to do with our day. Like before, only easier.

She is watching me to see if I'm going to vomit up my pills or my food.

This, I know.

'Linda is coming this morning, don't forget.' Mother talks at me, not to me.

  I don't have a list, but I remember anyway. Since I left hospital, I've been told to avoid writing lists. I can Live Life on my own, and Cope with new things.

Or so they say.

Linda arrives, and sits down. She still looks the same. Her saggy eyes look me over, and she says cheerfully, 'you're doing well, Allie!' I say 'yes.' because there isn't much else I can think of.

'Have you seen the therapist this week?'

'Yes'

'And how is that going? Hmm?'

I hate it when people **hmm** at me.

'Well, thank you'.

I say well, but I mean awful. I have to talk about things in my life, which I had thought I'd forgotten, but which I clearly haven't. The therapist made me talk about the crash and how I felt guilty.

Time Will Pass

Things Will Get Better

You'll Start To Feel Well Soon

There Are People Around You Who Love You

Never Feel Bad About How You Feel

Linda goes away happy, now that I am being cared for.

I never understood why people like her want to do a job where they have to deal with people like Me all day. People like Me. Who *are* people like Me?

Who?

Better than Why. I haven't heard Why in a while. I don't even ask myself Why...

I don't even ask myself Why.

*   *   *

Starting again is not something you can do unless you want to. And it is impossible to truly start again, because you are the still the same person.

Put the old life in a box.

This way, you can hide away the things that follow you around, like ghosts. Ghosts have no care as to who you are and how they make you feel. You have to take charge yourself. You have to tell them who is boss and that is why they can't hurt you.

I have no ghosts following me.

The Thin Commandments

Hannah Marie Davis

I have lived on this edge of existence for so long now that I know no other way. I have no **desire to live**; yet I do not have an overwhelming **desire to die**.

I must never allow myself to get fat again. **Ever**.

My wish is to weigh **80lbs**.

22nd June 2004

Today's intake:

Exercise - 40 minutes step machine, 40 minutes running

Breakfast – Half an apple

Lunch – 2 crackers with low fat spread

Dinner - An apple, some vegetables, small piece of meat

I've eaten so much today. I'm such a greedy pig. I am disgusting.

A moment on the lips, forever on the hips.

5th July 2004

Exercise - 200 crunches, 40 minutes step machine.

I have been so good for the last 3 days. I have fasted and for the first time ever managed to last three days!

Today's intake - **absolutely nothing!** Not even water.

The good news is that I got on the scales today and was down to 9llb. **My** lowest ever!

Bad news is that I passed out twice during my fast. Mum went mad the second time, forcing me to drink sweet tea, which marked the end of my fast. **Damn my mother**.

5th July 2004

Victoria passed out this morning after getting out of the bath. I was shocked by how thin she looked just wrapped in a towel. She has been losing weight again and hiding it from us. Anorexia makes her sneaky. I tried to get her to eat some breakfast but she just pushed the food round her plate.

We've been here before. Victoria has struggled with food for 4 years and has been hospitalized twice. Initially she just cut back on sugary foods, embarking on a healthier diet but gradually she ate less and less and became more and more withdrawn and sullen. I really thought she had recovered. I can't believe my baby might be ill again!

12th July 2004

Weight: 89lb. Yes!

Exercise - 40 minutes step machine, 40 minutes power walking. 122 crunches.

Breakfast - 1 slice of bread with a sliced boiled egg on top (mum forced me to eat and watched me like a hawk.)
Lunch – Nothing.
Dinner - A piece of chicken with steamed spinach and 2 tablespoons of peas.
Snacks - Handful of raisons.

I will be thin, I will be thin, I will be thin.

I have to lose that goddamn **11lb,** reach my goal weight. Once I am thin, I'll eat normally.

I just have to get thin first!

18th July 2004

Victoria has become so sullen. She is also lining everything up in her room and gets very upset if either Malcolm or I move any of her things. Our daughter is ill again. She seems much worse this time. Before, it was far easier to persuade her to eat but this time she is aggressive and confident that she doesn't need food. Victoria is refusing to be weighed and I think she is secretly visiting the gym when she should be in classes. Malcolm says it's time we made her an appointment with her therapist. I cannot believe that anorexia has got a grip over us once again.

24th July 2004

Victoria's therapist was shocked by her regression and physical state today. She immediately referred Victoria for a physical examination, which revealed she had lost a considerable amount of weight. Her doctor confirmed that she is suffering from anorexia again. They have recommended that she be admitted into hospital immediately to prevent her getting any worse. I cried myself to sleep.

BOURNEWOOD HOSPITAL

NAME: ROBINSON, VICTORIA   **PATIENT NO.** 31408

DATE: ADMISSION: 25/07/04, 86lbs

DISCHARGE: 24/08/04, 95lb

DISCHARGE SUMMARY

The patient is a 19 year old, white, intelligent, high achieving, single female with a four-year history of severe anorexia nervosa, with sporadic psychotic features including obsessive-compulsive behaviour. The patient has been treated at this unit before on several occasions with varying degrees of success. On her last discharge the patient was considered to be physically stabilised but behaviourally disordered. Her most recent stay followed a collapse at home.

PAST MEDICAL HISTORY: Appeared to be relatively healthy up until she began to show obsessive behaviour concerning studying and other cognitive obsessions.

FAMILY HISTORY: Only child. Relatively happy childhood. Extremely close to mother. Patient is very keen to impress both her parents through academic achievements.

HOSPITAL COURSE: Patient appeared to be cooperative. However, staff discovered the patient had been hiding food. Once this issue was resolved the patient gained weight at a steady rate. Seemed resentful of this weight gain but appreciated it was necessary.

LABORATORY TESTS AND VITAL SIGNS: Severely dehydrated and malnourished on admission with elevated calcium levels.

FINAL DIAGNOSIS: Severe Anorexia Nervosa.

       Obsessive-compulsive personality disorder.

       Prone to habitual relapse.

30th July 2004

The unit that Victoria is being treated in is one of the best in the country but it is so difficult to see her there. The unit specialises in treating people with eating disorders, like Victoria. The patients are locked on the ward and initially are not allowed to leave. They're not allowed phone calls or letters or even to write a diary, as their full focus should be on recovery. Eventually, after they have proven they are willing to co-operate they earn 'privileges' such as being allowed to go for walks, visits and eventually day release. Some members of the family have found this very hard to understand, comparing the unit to prison but the way in which Victoria's eating disorder is raging throughout her at the moment, I honestly do not think she would be able to cope at home.

7th[th] July 2004

Victoria seems to be making progress and the doctors have suggested bringing her home in a few days and putting her on the day-care programme to see how she copes. This would involve her going back to the unit for a few hours in the day and following a set meal plan. I truly hope this works.

24th August 2004

I came home today, which felt good but was horrified to discover that mum had rearranged my room and hidden the scales. Not only are all of my things in the wrong order but also I don't even know how fat those stupid doctors have made me! At least I can write my diary again now. It is so much easier to motivate myself when I can order my thoughts on a page.

I have to go to the unit everyday and follow their stupid meal plan, which contains about a zillion calories. What they don't know is that I'm getting very good at hiding food! Ha!

If I eat **anything, I'll eat everything and thus I can eat nothing!**

11th September 2004

I had a quick chat with Victoria's therapist today. She explained that anorexia often becomes part of the sufferer's identity. In a way, sufferers need it to cope with life; it becomes their friend, the one thing that never ever leaves them. She told me that we mustn't try and force Victoria's illness from her because at the moment she would not be able to cope without the order and control it affords her. I felt a little better after the phone call and although I had never thought about anorexia in this way, it did seem to make sense.

21st September 2004

Exercise - 60 minutes walking. 155 crunches.

I'm still having to follow that stupid meal plan and I **KNOW** I am getting fatter. Mum has agreed to let me walk to the unit. Silly her! As if I am going to go! I'll go to the gym and then into town to buy some scales! I don't need the unit.

Hunger is taught **and can be unlearned!**

22nd September 2004

Weight: 88lb. So **heavy**.

Exercise - 40 minutes step machine, 120 minutes power walking. 355 crunches.

Breakfast – Apple.
Lunch – Carrot sticks.
Dinner – 3 tablespoons of boiled rice with vegetables.

I am not sick. I know I am not sick because I am still so fat.

88lb scares me.

I am fully aware that anorexia has made me selfish. I cannot eat for the sake of my family despite their pleas. They cannot see the fat.

I need to be thin, I need to be thin.

My ideal weight is now **70lb**.

30th September 2004

The unit has called to say that Victoria hasn't been attended the day care centre for over a week. I knew nothing about it but it only means one thing… She is not getting better at all. We should have guessed. She is compulsively studying for hours at a time and insists on eating alone in her room. The signs were there, I just didn't want to see them. Malcolm has booked a crisis care meeting with her doctor and therapist tomorrow to discuss where we should go from here. I feel absolutely helpless.

1st October 2004

I am in control.

If I set my mind to it I can achieve whatever I want. I want to be **70lb**.

My food intake has been decreasing. The doctors have told me that my body needs 2000 calories a day to maintain a healthy weight. 2000! What do they know? I can function perfectly on 400 calories. My school grades are better than ever! I can study all night! Hunger keeps sleep away. I am not sick.

Ate 3 cookies but purged them all straight away. My new favourite trick! Chew 'n' throw!

I've also been fooling mum by drinking lots and lots of water before she weighs me. This makes both her and me happier as she believes I'm maintaining my weight and I just know it is water (no calories, no preservatives, no fat).

I am in control.

BOURNEWOOD HOSPITAL

NAME: ROBINSON, VICTORIA   **PATIENT NO.** 31408

DATE: ADMISSION: 11/10/04

ADMISSION SUMMARY

The patient is a 19 year-old female, with a history of severe anorexia nervosa. Admitted after substantial coercion by her care team and parents.

Appears to be extremely emaciated; initial weigh-in indicated the patient weighed 82lb - water loading is suspected.

Determined not to cooperate. Seems to have lost the will to recover. Potentially suicidal through continued and prolonged fasting.

HOSPITAL COURSE: Close monitoring required. To be given 3 meals a day plus two snacks and frequent fluids. If the patient refuses to cooperate at meal times she should be given a can of Ensure (300 calories) under supervision. No unsupervised bathroom trips for two hours following each meal as her mother suspects vomiting.

VITAL SIGNS: Severely malnourished. Eyes contain several burst blood vessels, knuckles are grazed which indicate frequent vomiting.

14th October 2004

I am so worried. Victoria is completely despondent and doesn't even talk when I visit. She is painfully thin; her legs are struggling to hold her. Her hair is dirty and unwashed, there is a fur creeping all over her and her teeth are beginning to rot because she vomits so much. I'm struggling to recognize my bright, bubbly daughter. Anorexia has robbed her of everything and both Malcolm and I are powerless to help her. Victoria has never been this bad before. She seems driven to death.

BOURNEWOOD HOSPITAL

NAME: ROBINSON, VICTORIA   **PATIENT NO.** 31408

DATE: 19/10/04

PROGRESS SUMMARY

Patient has lost a further 5lb. Refuses to eat at meal times; water loads before weigh-in and has been caught hiding food. Vital signs degenerating. Passing out frequently. Has been put on bed rest.

Recommendation is that she is tube fed for a minimum of 1 week in order to stabilise her weight. Patient is refusing to consent to treatment.

26th October 2004

Victoria is desperately ill. She keeps passing out yet won't consent to being tube fed. As she is over 18 it is her decision. Once again, Malcolm and I are completely powerless as we watch our beloved little girl dice with death. I feel so desperately useless. Victoria will not even talk to us, let alone let us help her or hug her. She's is so lost in her own little world and there appears to be no way of reaching through to her. Please, please, let this end.

BOURNEWOOD HOSPITAL

NAME: ROBINSON, VICTORIA   **PATIENT NO.** 31408

DATE: 27/10/04

PROGRESS SUMMARY

Patient displaying oppositional behaviour. Refusing to meet expectations of unit. Cannot treat without relevant consent. Expressed a wish to discharge herself.

FINAL DIAGNOSIS Grave longstanding anorexia with bulimic tendencies.

>Severely malnourished.

>Body self-cannibalising in an attempt to maintain itself.

>Critically ill: in state of malnutrition, danger to life.

28th October 2004

I cannot believe Victoria has discharged herself! It feels like I am bringing her home to die. I am so angry with her yet at the same time want to wrap her in cotton wool and tell her everything will be OK. She did not have the strength to walk to the car; Malcolm had to push her in a wheelchair. The doctors have asked us to consider having her sectioned under the Mental Health Act but that seems so final and desperate. We are at our wits' end and do not know which way to turn. We are just praying that now she is home something fundamental shifts in her and she rediscovers the will to live.

1st November 2004

Weight: 70lb.

Exercise – 122 leg lifts in bed

Breakfast – Nothing

Lunch – Carrot sticks.

Dinner – Rice and vegetables.

I'm getting closer to being invisible. Tomorrow I shall start a fast. Mum keeps crying but she doesn't understand. I want to tell her but she will think I am crazy.

MY THIN COMMANDMENTS:

1. Thin equals pretty.

2. Being thin is more important than being alive and fat.

3. Thou shall take laxatives, purge all that is eaten and starve oneself.

4. Thou shall not eat without feeling guilty.

5. Thou shall count calories and restrict intake accordingly.

6. Thou shall not eat fattening food without punishing oneself afterwards.

7. Thou shall weigh oneself throughout the day.

8. Thou shall never gain weight.

9. Thou can never be too thin.

10. Not eating is a sign of true success.

Anorexia is my new religion!

7th November 2004

Weight: 68lb.

Exercise - 60 minutes power walking.

Breakfast – Apple
Lunch – 3 cups of black coffee.

Dinner – Boiled rice and ham.

Everyday is such a battle. My skin feels so tight. I just want to take it off.
So tired now. Tired of food, tired of treatment, tired of me, tired of my life.

Why feed a body that doesn't want to live?

12th November 2004

Weight: 66lb.

Today's intake: NOTHING!

I have decided to not eat or drink a thing. Everything becomes so much
simpler when you take food out of the equation. I'm starving my body of
food but my head is flooded with it. I think about food every minute of
every day. My head is imploding. I can't cope anymore. If I get so close
to death that it seems inevitable, maybe I can choose to live but at the
moment living is not an option. Fasting is the way forward for now, the
only solution I can think of.

Simple. Straightforward. Easy.

13th November 2004

Victoria seems to be pushing herself further than ever before. She told a
close friend that she wanted to hover as near to death as possible and then
choose to live rather than have it forced upon her. This obviously worried
her friend who called me immediately. It initially sent me into a crazed

panic, thinking she was on some hell bent suicide attempt. But, as

Malcolm pointed out, this is the first time she has mentioned living since she fell ill this time and surely we must take this as a positive. I'm not sure. We've scheduled a meeting with her doctors tomorrow.

16th November 2004

Weight: 64lb.

Today's intake: NOTHING!

I'm so tired. Not sure I can do it anymore but then if **starving was**

easy, everyone would do it.

18th December 2004

Last month was the worst month of my life. Victoria collapsed at home and we couldn't bring her round. When the ambulance arrived the paramedics said that her heart was struggling. She was rushed straight into hospital where she was tube fed and ventilated. She remained unconscious for three days. Malcolm and I just sat watching the drips, hoping they would feed life back into her drop by drop. When she finally opened her eyes and we explained what had happened she cried and cried and cried letting us hug her for the first time in months. She said that she didn't want to die and that she wanted to fight back against anorexia. At last, the change in her perspective has come! I'm daring to hope we'll be able to have a relatively normal Christmas together if the doctors deem her fit even to come home.

27ᵗʰ December 2004

I don't want food to stay inside me and I do not want to eat. I still want to lose weight. But I do not want to be frightened of going to sleep in case my heart stops and I don't wake up, or frightened of going in the shower in case I pass out. One of the other girls from the unit wrote and told me that she knew someone with anorexia who stopped eating when she was released and her heart stopped. She was the same age as me. I can't let this happen to me. I have to try to get better. I don't want my heart to stop.

11ᵗʰ January 2005

I've started attending the unit during the day again now I am well enough. I've been having long chats with my therapist and am finally starting to try and understand 'me' and why I've got anorexia. I think I became anorexic because I had **lost my voice**. At first it wasn't about getting thin. It was more about being **noticed** for the right reasons and fitting in with all of the other girls at school. I always felt so out of place with them. Anorexia gave me back my voice; my thinness spoke volumes for me. My therapist thinks I am doing well and reminds me I only have to do things **one step at a time**. I won't lie, food still petrifies me but I'm trying to face my fear.

15ᵗʰ January 2005

I have just **eaten a full meal**. I shan't list it as that is negative behaviour, nor will I write in my weight anymore. I am trying not to focus on the food inside me but I can't help being scared. My breathing has quickened, my palms are sweaty and my chest feels tight. Anorexics don't eat. I feel like I've achieved something **huge** (eaten a full meal) and **failed** miserably all at the same time. I think I'm going to watch TV to take my mind off it.

7ᵗʰ **March 2005**

I am so proud of Victoria. She is still in the local hospital being monitored but will hopefully be coming home next week and shall just attend the unit in the daytime. This is great news as we thought she would have to be transferred back to the unit on a full time basis but her therapists think she is able to cope at home. She is smiling more now and attempting to eat something solid at each meal. It is clear that this still frightens her as she goes very quiet and has to give her full attention to the plate in front of her but it is progress and for that we are immensely grateful. I feel like my girl is on her way back to me!

21ˢᵗ **March 2005**

I ate my first meal in public today but purged it in the toilets afterwards. It was just too much to keep inside me. **Why did I do it?** I was doing so well. Maybe I am a failure after all. I'm so cross at myself!

24ᵗʰ **March 2005**

I told my therapist about me purging the other day. By the time I finished telling her I was crying and shouting because I was so cross with myself. I've not purged since and my therapist said not to beat myself up about it. It is how I dealt with it now that is important and I'm desperate not to get ill again. We went out together for a meal in the restaurant just by the clinic. I didn't have pudding or a starter but I ate the entire main course and didn't purge afterwards. With my therapist's support, I didn't feel the need to rush to the toilet or jog frantically around the park in a bid to 'lose' the calories I had consumed. Instead, as we walked along we told jokes and laughed. She said that she was proud of me and that made me so happy. I'm not going to get better, I'm getting better and it feels good!

Empty

Nickie Barrett

Facing the unknown: Tara's Story.

The future looked bright; good job with good prospects and now a place of my own, 'well a room', but a start and just the thing I needed to boost my independence. I'd been asked to house share with two other friends and I couldn't be more delighted. I was now seizing adult life by the horns and boy I was going to have a good time! They weren't particularly close friends, but I knew them well enough to feel I'd made the right decision. Marsha was fun, ambitious and loved Chinese food. She had an unhealthy desire for shoes, which did concern me a little over storage arrangements; I couldn't help wondering would there be any room for my stuff? She could also be fussy, arrogant and hell when she couldn't have a cigarette, but I was prepared to take a chance. The positive side was freedom to do as I pleased and I couldn't afford it any other way. Then there was Saffron; she was Marsha's friend rather than mine and I only knew her from odd occasions when she had tagged along on a night out. She would not be heard of for months then she'd appear like a phoenix rising from the ashes, glamorous with dark sultry looks, the perfect image of the girl that had everything, but Saffron hid a secret that often pulled her into the depths of despair. This often left her so low, that she would take to her bed for days, sometimes weeks. She would build her own space, turning her room into a safety net against the world, emerging only to use the bathroom and locking herself in for hours on end.

In the beginning, Saffron's mood swings were hard to accept, but gradually my other housemate and I (including visiting friends), began to read the pattern of events like an unfolding story. We took it in our stride to try to understand her and some of her strange routines. These would eventually encroach on her character. We came to know what would happen next, but despite this there were still times when she surprised us with her strange collective hiding habits. The hiding habits never ceased to amaze me; she would go to great lengths to hide food in sometimes the most obscure places. Once I found a packet of biscuits in the lampshade in the lounge, I was changing the bulb and they dropped out on me as I tried to stay balanced on the kitchen stool. It can hurt you know, being hit with a falling packet of custard creams from a great height! The airing cupboard was another place where food was often hidden: you'd grab a towel and a selection of pork pies and scotch eggs would tumble out. But this became the norm and although there were still the odd surprises, we tried to understand our friend's cry for help.

I can still remember the day I sensed all was not well in Saffron's world. It began when I needed the bathroom for a shower after work and after trying the door, a quiet voice from behind it told me they wouldn't be long. Understatement of the century! Three quarters of an hour later Saffron emerged, I remember looking at her, noticing her complexion and the beads of sweat that covered her face. Her eyes bore dark rings underneath, certainly not the picture of a freshly showered individual. My reaction said it all as she felt it necessary to explain that she felt unwell and was sorry for being so long. I asked her whether there was anything I could do. She shook her head and shuffled back to her room slowly. She reminded me of a delicate old lady, her frame crumpled and hunched in her long dressing gown. The famous dressing gown, this dressing gown was the symbol that told us when Saffron was 'ill'. She would never be out of the thing. It signified her comfort blanket; probably looking back it was something that made her feel secure and cosy from the outside world. For us, it was the difficulty of not understanding the truth and not knowing how to help.

Meal times were never a routine; we all had such different patterns that we just did our own thing. Marsha ate when she was hungry. The evening meal scene was out of the window with her. She wouldn't know the difference between a saucepan and a frying pan. Despite this unhealthy eating pattern she always looked amazing. She probably has the metabolism of a gazelle, I only had to look at a crispy fried pork ball and I would gain ten inches. Saffron often remarked on Marsha's svelte figure. She had an obsession of watching her eat; giving a running commentary on every morsel that got hooked onto her fork. I became increasingly uneasy with this behaviour. I would scuttle off to my room to eat my meals, which were generally not interesting. But I didn't relish the thought of being interrogated about the

brand of salad cream I'd used, or how many times I'd chew my food before I would allow myself to swallow. Food had become an obsession in this house. We had all fallen victim to Saffron's eating disorder.

Bulimia was an illness that I knew little about, but our housemate was in full throws of this illness and we couldn't ignore it. She had little contact with her father who she rowed with constantly. Her mother had died when she was a young child and her sister went on never ending back-packing trips, disappearing for months on end. It was a wet Friday in May that finally brought it home to me how much Saffron needed our help, anybody's help! After months of piling on the weight and then losing it again, brought on by constant days of throwing up, Saffron had got to her confident stage. There seemed to be a mid way point that she seemed to reach, one might call it the 'in between stage', I called it *party time*. This stage was when she looked and felt her best and this is when all her inhibitions were locked away. The real Saffron came out to party. Party she did, there was no stopping her and the men…. a constant stream of one night stands would drift in and out of our house. During this time you never knew who you might bump into on the way to the bathroom of a morning. Scuttling across the landing you would often bump into some bleary eyed, embarrassed looking guy as you both made a run for the loo for that first wee of the morning. It was more often than not that Saffron would not even know the name of her catch, grunting a very embarrassed goodbye as they left. Saffron needed help, she was a danger to herself, not only her health, but her pride and dignity too and she had sunk so low she was past the point of no return.

The morning after the night before was always an uncomfortable one; Saffron would emerge from her room still worse for wear, silent and shamefully embarrassed. I thought about how I would approach her.

   'Look,' I began. 'You've got to be careful, Saff, you don't know who you're bringing home, they could be a mass murderer!' I sat down on the couch next to her, waiting for some kind of reaction, but all she could do was sit dumbstruck, her wide eyes staring ahead, transparent and very empty as if she had no soul. We sat like this for a while and then Saffron spoke.

   'I don't know why I behave the way I do,' she said in a quiet voice. 'It's like my body gets taken over and I can't control it.' I looked at her; she looked almost childlike as she searched my face for some kind of answers.

'Saff, you have to get help for your illness, you can't go on like this.' Before I could even get the last words out, Saffron's head snapped round to look at me.

'What?' she snarled.

'Well you need some help.' I repeated. Saffron was enraged by my concern.

'I need no such thing, I can look after myself and I make my own decisions. Who the hell do you think you are poking your nose into my business? We share the rent but that gives you no right to nursemaid me!' With that, Saffron got up and stomped out of the lounge, knocking over two coffee cups as she went. I tried to shout after her that I was only looking out for her, but the bedroom door slammed shut so hard it knocked the George Michael calendar off the wall. It laid folded in half, so there was just George's eyes looking at me as if to say what a mess I'd made of that one.

Cookie Monster: Saffron's Story.

Binging and purging had started to take over my life. I felt I'd developed a knack of eating in a normal way in front of my friends, really just the odd nibble to give the impression I was in control of my food habits. As soon as I was on my own I turned into a food junkie devouring anything remotely edible. I didn't mean that lightly, I meant anything. When the binge attacks came I just had to stuff as much food into my mouth that was humanly possible. Any food was not a problem. I didn't wait for instant mixes to blend; they went straight down out of the packet, most of the powder going in my hair as well as my mouth. An example of a single binge attack could consist of a whole cooked chicken, three tubs of coleslaw, five sticks of pepperoni, a loaf of bread, two packets of custards creams, a tub of Dairylea and four sausage rolls. This could vary if I was on a roll and the food was instantly obtainable. I suppose you could say I'd developed a routine and the more I did it the more cunning I became, hiding food, hiding the truth, living the ultimate lie. Life had become a challenge in every sense of the word. No matter how much I craved to be 'normal', I knew at this present time it was as unlikely as pigs flying south for the winter; the ironic thing was, that I hid my eating disorder far too well, so well, that no one around me ever felt the need to challenge me or make me stop!

I've always been impulsive, even as a child and maybe thinking back, that is where it all started. Snap decisions to do stuff often led me into a load of trouble. But nothing was more impulsive than the decision to cleanse my body from the evil stuff called food that I adored so much. I was obsessed with breakfast, dinner and tea. My sister on the other hand was not. She looked like the ballerina doll that you find on the top of those musical boxes that aunts always buy for Christmas and birthdays. She never cared much for mealtimes; she ate because it was a function to survive. Not like me, I ate because food had become an obsession. It was a comfort and while I ate it gave me a few moments to keep busy. This allowed me to forget the hurt of always trying to compete with my perfect sister. Wish Mum was here, miss her so much.

I can remember the first time I did it. I felt shame that I had little left on my plate after the huge Christmas dinner aunt Margaret had laid on. Relatives looked on, congratulating me on my triumph, patting me on the back for the effort I'd put in.

'That's the way Saffy, we can always rely on you.'

Uncle Ken looked approvingly as my plate was taken away.

'Your sister never quite finishes hers though; I've seen more meat on a sparrow.'

I so wanted to look like a sparrow, instead I was the child whose belly always got prodded to the words of my father,

'Here she is my chunky little bundle.'

It was then I knew I had to get thin. I had to get the extra food I had eaten out. It wasn't easy sticking your fingers down your throat. You gag, your eyes water, your throat becomes sore, but I soon developed putrid cocktails to help the experience. I knew that my stomach was well and truly empty; you could see that by the contents of the toilet bowl. My theory now was, I could eat whatever I liked and not feel guilty for it. It was, for me, the solution I'd been looking for, an easy way of consuming the food I enjoyed then cleansing my body of any trace. I was going to be that ballerina doll.

Releasing the demon: Marsha's Story.

Saffron had been my friend since primary school; she hadn't had an easy childhood. I always remember the chaotic family life that Saffron came from. Her Mum had become seriously ill when we were seven years old and that September she passed away. Her Dad did the best he could and tried to protect Saffron and her younger sister from the world, but would always seem to shelter Saffron's sister more. Saffron always had to watch out for her sister. We would often walk her to one of her many out of school activities that her Dad had encouraged. As I think back, I recall the lack of attention poor Saff had. This now accounts for a lot of the insecurities that I noticed in Saffron over the years. She became so critical of herself; it was very hard to snap her out of the self-loathing for her own body. She would miss out on endless school trips, discos and shopping trips with friends. I knew then she had a problem, but I was just too immature to realise the extent of it.

Sharing a house with Saff was something we had decided we'd do long before leaving school. We used to dream of our own place and spend hours describing how we'd decorate. However, moving in with Saffy was so different to what I imagined. Her strange habits soon led me to believe that she was ill and not just eccentric. I began to smell vomit, not just occasionally but all the time. I'd always had an acute sense of smell, my noble nose had to account for some good I suppose. I tackled my housemates about this but both denied it, although I was aiming at one rather than the other. I'd noticed the wrappers, the missing food and the smell of burgers at three in the morning. I knew Saff had some sort of problem but confronting her was going to be difficult. I cared deeply for Saff, I didn't want to hurt her, I'd always been taught to respect the privacy of others. Several times I had started to talk to Saffron, but it was as though she knew the next line and would change the subject at phenomenal speed. All of a sudden we would be talking about how too much chlorine had been put into the local swimming pool, or next door's pigeon collection.

I struggled with the battle of confronting my friend with her problem, until one day when I came home from work. It was lunchtime, I'd had a crappy day and my head was splitting. I'd decided that after lunch I just couldn't face going back to work. I got to the front of the house and put my key in the door. The door would not budge; I rattled the key around and discovered the latch was on. I called out, as I knew Saffron was home.

'Saff,' I shouted through the letterbox.

A stifled voice came back at me.

'Hang on a minute,' she shouted back.

'Hurry up I'm bursting for the loo,' I replied with crossed legs.

Not being able to wait any longer I ran through the side entry round to the back of the house and in through the garden gate. I tried the back door, which was also locked, so I peered in through the kitchen window. Inside the kitchen was laden with food items. I didn't know we had that much food in the house. It was then that I noticed half this stuff was open; packets lay strewn across the work surfaces like an invasion of squirrels had taken over the house. I then craned my neck and saw Saff frantically trying to clean it up. I knocked the window and Saffy looked round in dismay. She wearily let me in the back door. We looked at each other; her face was like that of an animal caught in the headlights of a car.

'I...' Saffron tried to speak.

'I know Saff,' I put my arms out to her. 'I figured all along it was something like this, you're bulimic aren't you?' I asked in a softened tone. Saffron fell towards my outstretched arms and wept. She cried so hard, as though the feeling of sheer relief swept through her.

'Why didn't you tell me Saff? You knew I was here for you, all this sneaking and secrecy. It's no good.'

'I couldn't tell anyone, it's what I do, I have to do this on my own,' Saffron sobbed.

'This is killing you Saffy, you need to get professional help,' I tried to sound strong. I knew I needed to get tough, for Saffron's sake. That night the hurt and pain that Saffron had held in for so long all came flooding out. The need to talk was something she needed so badly. It was as though a tonne weight had been lifted off her shoulders and just to share the huge secret that she had lived with for ten years was a huge release. In the coming weeks I had convinced Saffron to see the GP and she knew this was her first port of call, the first step on a long rocky road. After this there were numerous appointments and between us, Tara and I would accompany Saffron. She needed all the support we could give and it also helped us fully understand the disease. Saffron's first treatment was an anti vomiting drug; this reduced the binging and purging incidents by half. When Saffron felt a binging incident coming on, rather than isolating herself she would eat in front of us. This according to her Psychotherapist was the first sign of success to curing her compulsion. Facing her demons was another and back tracking the root of her problem became another therapeutic tool. This it seemed was going to be a long slow process but I would make sure I'd be there for her.

New Beginning: Saffron's story.

I had been told I had to accept myself for who I was. I knew the key to all this lay with my father's acceptance of me. If he could stop comparing me to my sister then this would be a start. I had to analyse my behaviour and ask myself, do I really want the 2.30am binges and the feeling of total loneliness. I did have choices, I was strong and I could beat this. I can't say I'm cured, what is cured? I will always be bulimic; getting better is how I would describe it. For the time being I still think I need to have blinkers on when I go to the local shop, just so I can't see the sweet counter or the cake display. So what, I am meant to be voluptuous and my sister is stick thin. That's just the way it is. We are all different and have to accept who we are. We are all individuals. I'm me; I don't want to hide it. I want to live it, as Saffron.

Hope

Emma Vryenhoef

Settled at the square dining table of a cosy flat two women talked, both in their late fifties but heads bent close together like conspiratorial teenagers. A lagging but comfortable silence had enveloped the two as the discussion paused for them to push aside their now empty mugs and lean back into their chairs.

'You should write a book,' Sarah began, venturing onto a new avenue of conversation.

'Me? Why?' Maggie scoffed.

'You've had an interesting life…'

'You make it sound like its over. Besides, why would anyone want to hear about me,' she was well aware of the answer to this but continued anyway, 'it's so self-indulgent?'

'Because,' Sarah ploughed on taking a deep breath, 'when we first found out you had MS I didn't know anything about it, none of us did.'

'So I'm to write a handbook then, 'How to Battle Multiple Sclerosis,' something inspirational' she raised her right hand, shaping out an imaginary banner in the air, her left hand sat shaking upon her lap.

'Maggie, you know what I meant, you make it sound depressing.'

'It is…'

'Not always...'

The words hung there as Maggie tried to decipher whether it was a statement or a question. At times like these the numbness in her left leg seemed to magnify, tauntingly reminding her of the truth.

'No, not always but that's what people want to hear isn't it, something tragic. Nothing about shifting that extra stone I gained after the kids, or getting to spend all my time on my art rather than a stressful job.'

'Stop it Mags I'm trying to be serious.'

'So am I', she retorted sharply. Part of her missed the ability to run away, the dramatic ending to an awkward discussion was robbed from her though, so she recovered with the only reasonable thing she could think of, an apology. 'Sorry I'm in a foul mood at the moment, seeing David tomorrow and everything.'

'I know, but think about what he says Maggie, he only wants the best for you.'

That night Maggie took out her Dictaphone usually used to expound some of her literary theories and began uncertainly to talk about her day.

Something Sarah had said had made her think and now that tiny thought had

grown and all day she had been imagining what she would say if she were
to record a book.

'A little late in the day to be reciting this, I should have begun
sooner. I never thought I had anything to say and now, perhaps, for a first
in my life, lack of time has become a problem.' Maggie stopped the tape,
feeling ridiculous, doubting the value of her friend's words, but as she
considered this, something sparked inside her mind.

'I guess I hadn't the heart to tell Sarah I couldn't write anymore,
especially after her tirade on the uselessness of chip and pin cards earlier.
To me they're a Godsend, as far as I know and that's not a lot. I'll still
remember that little four-digit number that guarantees me some
independence even after my speech becomes slurred. I guess the Braille
bumps will help when my eyesight gets worse too.

I used to try everyday to write out the alphabet, on the instructions
of my doctor, since apparently it would help. I felt like I shouldn't, but I
gave up in the end, much to his disapproval. Everyone is obsessed with me
being as normal as possible. But, after all the paperwork was sorted out by
Richard when I was first diagnosed, all filed away awaiting my death like
it's tomorrow or just around the corner, writing didn't seem all that
important anymore. I'd rather be able to walk and that takes enough practice.
I could see the hours of my day falling away before me while I worked to
retain my motor functions, going through exercises one at a time. I missed
living.

*   *   *

The day had finally come for Maggie and her son, David, to have
lunch but it was full of dread for both of them. The same argument seemed
to replay itself between them, neither hearing what the other said, two
mirrors reflecting each other's flaws.

'How are you going to cope on your own though?' David questioned
roughly.

'Well, when your father died and I didn't have any reason to get up
in the morning, no one to bring coffee to first thing, I got the cat...' she
replied, knowing full well that he would not wait long enough for her to
elaborate.

'Mum this isn't the same, another cat, dog, rabbit, whatever, is not going to solve anything.'

'I don't want another cat; I'm trying to make a point. I'll find another way to deal with this, just like I always do. Things work out David.'

'No they don't. You can't rely on positive thinking to make it OK, it's ridiculous.'

'It's already OK.'

'What are you talking about?'

Here it came, the news they both knew was going to pop out, the one thing that David did not want to hear and the reason behind his organisation of a 'talk' with his mother. He wanted her to be looked after, so Maggie made a pre-emptive strike.

'I've found a small flat, its better for me; there are no steps, it's closer for Jenny.'

'Oh Christ Mother! Why does it matter how far your cleaning lady has to walk!'

'It's not for her, it's for me.'

'Then why don't you move near to us or Mike?'

'I like where I live, it's where my friends are and I've always been there since before you were born.'

'Things will have to change, at least give me and Mike a key so we can check up on you, just in case.'

'Look, I like my life. I like my privacy, I like the cleaning done my way and I like Jenny doing it. I like to cook my own food and I like to wander around my own house naked.' David raised his eyebrows unconsciously in surprise. 'Yes David, your mother dances around the house naked listening to Miles Davis! Now, do you still want a key?'

David sat sulkily, resenting his mother's flippant attitude to her illness. Maggie adjusted her scarlet scarf, feeling suffocated.

The next morning Maggie cringed remembering the horrid goodbye and the restless tension that emanated from her relationship with her eldest son. It had not gone well, but then again it never did. Sighing in irritation, she looked about her room, decorated in beautiful vibrant paintings. She hated to leave her dear little flat. But after all paintings could be moved, she would colonise somewhere else and it would be just as homely as she had made this place. Looking at her artwork, a memory came to her so she reached across stiffly for the Dictaphone, an action that had become habit in the last few days.

'I remember shortly after I was diagnosed I found a picture, it was one of many self-portraits I had attempted in my early thirties and I was trying to reconcile what I saw with the woman who gazed back at me in the mirror. But what I saw there was the same steady clear eyes and high cheekbones. I had loved the velvet feel of charcoal and the scratching tones of graphite but I never bothered trying to draw again after that day, knowing that I would be unable to surpass the minute detail of the image in front of me, that the gradual loss of my finer functions would just frustrate me. Some people, after all, have never been able to draw, so I took up paint and ink and began massaging it into the page. And then I began to hang them round the house displaying my garish, brilliant new direction, my rejection that apparently I was dying.'

The alarm clock suddenly interrupted Maggie's words; it was undoubtedly time for her to get up. With a great sigh and more than a little effort she swung her legs out over the side of the bed, tenderly rubbing her knees in ginger anticipation of the weight of her body on unsteady feet. Her left side still shook, there was nothing to make it cease but she looked forward to her massage therapy before lunch, it was the small things that made a difference. Taking the paper to Mrs Beatty, three doors down, was part of a weekly routine and this Sunday was no different than those in the last twenty-five years.

The final few steps to Mrs Beatty's green front door seemed, to Maggie, much harder than they should have been. A great rushing descended on her, a waterfall, filling her ears and emptying her mind. Looking up to identify the vast thundering, endlessness, she felt weary. The light of midday approaching, the imaginary spray seemed to twinkle like a thousand tiny stars in front of her eyes. Waiting in the street, yearning for the moisture to blanket her upturned face, Maggie began to shake. A silent blackness descended, dancing around the pricks of brightness that were. Too hot, not the cold loneliness that escaping should be. Suddenly Maggie became heavy, elbow, and shoulders, every angle jarred to the earth as she fell, a crumpled puppet.

*   *   *

As she lay there motionless and silent David tried to imagine how any of the small, meagre figures surrounding the bed would have looked in her place, engulfed in the vast crisp whiteness of hospital linen. Maggie's imposing form was shrunken, bundled up, restricted and posed. A false sleep, so unlike the natural sprawl of rest. An uneasy silence blankets the room. It seemed rude to ask about work, about what people have done all day, what they do when they are not here. From the bed her eyes flicker open, wander from face to face, to thin air and then to something beyond all of them. Expectant expressions fail and the quiet grew more oppressive. Breaking the silence, David begins,

'It's freezing out; I can't believe how fast the weather changes.'

'I know,' the voice of his brother echoed agreement, 'and the mist too, it's awful. There've been loads of accidents on the ring road.'

'Beautiful this morning though, crisp… ' David's voice died away as he noticed her cold blue eyes fall from the window into sleep. The weather was always a poor excuse for conversation in his mother's view. A quiet relief swept the room; everyone more than ready to take up their papers, books and crosswords once more.

The blinding light of waking was like the birth of a star; a supernova like the ones explained in some of the tomes that adorned Maggie's plethora of rickety bookshelves at home. Her eyes fluttered to the window, everything was so still except the mocking lashes in their butterfly movement, opening and closing their delicate wings on her face. Lying there exhausted, relaxing into the linen and surrounded by comfortingly aching parts of herself, Maggie knew that she could not move her legs, despite the vague feeling in them which deceptively promised recovery.

Sitting down, watching her breathing slowly, steadily descending into sleep David lost himself in thought. To him the MS was like building a dam of sand against the tide; each time you fall back you lose a precious bit of ground. There is no battle, no war. It is a betrayal. His mother's body refused to fight and not only that, it began to destroy itself. Ever since he first knew, he had researched, investigated, cut out from newspapers every little bit of knowledge to piece together an understanding. Deciphering medical textbooks, or at least trying and processing all that information still brought him to the conclusion that Multiple Sclerosis was a betrayal. A malfunction of human genetics, the immune system, viruses, they are all chance elements that happen to collide. Although he knew that it wasn't his mother's fault, there was something unpleasant in his head, which taunted him with the idea that she was implicit in it. He had no notion of what happened next, no matter how many books he read, he had to quickly learn that the end is something never described. MS is not a terminal illness.

*   *   *

Rifling through the dressing table, David packed only what he thought necessary to Maggie's comfort, many skirts and books lay abandoned in a box at the foot of her double bed, marked for the charity shop. Moving to the bedside table he felt an uncomfortable pang as he reached to open the draw, everything was so still, so perfect as if she would return at a moments notice, lead by that all knowing presence that only a mother can have. Hand cream, Parma-violets, and a handkerchief, the air from the draw made him smile, it was her scent. He remembered as a child rummaging through her bag in search of the sweets. Dejectedly he let his weight fall on the bed beside him, fingering the handkerchief gently he tucked it in his trouser pocket. Fumbling with the sweet wrapper, his large fingers a far cry from the secret stealth of the child he once was, he placed a violet on his tongue and sat in silence letting the flavour fill his head. Pocketing the sweets and hand cream as well, he bent down a little to peer into the draw. At the back laid a Dictaphone, hidden from the light that loomed in as the low-slung sun cast its rays through the window. Rewinding it just a little, for the whirring seemed immense in the emptiness and then he began to listen.

'I remember the stooping doctor already crumpled with years of study and the weight of his work on his back, he said that I,' David stopped the tape, cutting off his mother's voice, then winding it forward a little he began it again, 'I remember when Richard died.' Immediately his father's name stirred his grim uneasy curiosity within him, he let the tape continue.

'The strange thing was that I couldn't shake the feeling, as all those familiar eyes rested on me, that my reaction was being judged, that somehow they all thought it should have been me they were burying and that in my face they'd see that same emotion reflected, one of guilt and regret that it wasn't me in that coffin. It was funny. Richard had once said he wanted to be the first to go, that he couldn't bear the thought of going on without me here and he'd go ahead and make the place shipshape for my arrival…bless his soul. I knew it then, that day when David sat me at the front of the church, a good caring son, I knew then what I'd become.' There was a long pause as David heard his mother take in a deep lonely breath, lost in her private thoughts.

'I am a pariah, literally, metaphorically, it all makes sense. I looked up at the face of Jesus, strung out in what could be life or death peering down at the pews and I just knew. All the family followed Richard in as he was held aloft by David and Michael and his friends and I sat there waiting for him to come to me, waiting for the sluggish pace of my dead husband to outstrip me. I remember how hard I was shaking, I was so angry, but people only saw the quivering frame of the MS. And that was it. That was the awkward and askew frame that everyone saw me in, even my own sons… my own boys. No one can see this as any sort of life they'd want, I'm sure they all wonder why I don't let strangers into my house to take care of me or go into a home somewhere, why I don't just die. I've never envied Richard anything in an entire lifetime but the peace he found that day, not death, just that when he went he wasn't fussed over, cosseted, coddled, controlled, treated like a child…that's all.'

The voice stopped and the crackle of the tape told him another entry was about to begin but he didn't need to hear anymore. The Dictaphone felt like a brick in his hand. She had sounded defeated and it was because of him, not the MS.

David's down cast eyes flickered on the box at the end of his mother's bed and shame welled up with the tears in his eyes. Angrily he wiped them away with the back of his hand and sprang into action. Upturning the box onto the bed, he began to refold the clothes into neat piles then sorted through the books he had previously discarded; he found two that he knew would spark his mother's interest. Placing them in a bag with some clean clothes and the Dictaphone, he knew it was time to head back to the hospital.

Part Two: Death

Living with Dying

Naomi Alsop

Saturday 7th January 2006

Seven bloody days into the New Year and already things are getting worse. I've tried everything I can think of to knock some sense into her but she won't bloody listen. I've pleaded, I've cajoled, I've shouted, but she's given up. She's decided to die.

She's been in a really funny mood today, hardly talking to me and monosyllabic when she does. Then this evening something seemed to snap in her. She's been on the sofa all day watching TV so I took her meal through for her. She sat there looking up at me as I held her tray.

'Here's your dinner.' I smiled at her as she stared at me. She didn't respond so I tried to balance the plate on the table next to her.

'You are good to me' she said. Her face was cold and speculative.

I forced out a laugh and attempted a smile. 'Well it's all good practice for when we have kids!' I regretted it before I had finished the sentence. I knew I needed to get out of there, but as I turned to escape I caught sight of the contempt in her face and hesitated for a moment, a rabbit before a lorry.

'I can't do this any more.' Her voice was hushed, but it cut at me across the room.

'I'll turn it off then.' I replied warily, knowing she wouldn't be so easily diverted. 'I'm not surprised, really. You've been watching it all day.'

For a moment she looked at me blankly as if I'd spoken a foreign language, then suddenly her face screwed up and she threw herself back in her chair.

'Not the telly!' she bit at me. 'This!' Her hand jabbed at the space between us. 'I can't keep *lying* like this. I can't keep up the pretence.' She looked at me and groaned, her shoulders drooping. 'Spence, this is no good. You've *got* to accept that I can't win this fight.' She paused, waiting for a reaction, but I couldn't speak. 'I'm *dying*, Spence. The doctors have *told* us that they can't cure me. The cancer is terminal. I'm going to die. There's nothing anyone can *do* now.'

My teeth clenched and the words hissed out. 'The doctors have been wrong before.'

'Not *this* time. I can feel it. I'm dying.'

I couldn't speak for what felt like an eternity. I could feel the anger bubbling up from the place in my stomach where I'd been hiding it. When my voice forced itself out of me I barely recognised it; it was high-pitched and strangled.

'So that's it then, is it? The doctors tell you you're going to die, so you decide you'd better be a good little patient? After all the fighting we've done together? After all the things I've done for you, everything I've given up for you? After all you've *fucking* put me through.' I was standing over her, shouting into her face. 'What the *hell* was the *point* of it all if you're just going to give up and die?' I left, slamming the door so hard the windows shook in their frames.

Monday 23ʳᵈ January 2006

What have I become? All the assumptions I made about how I would respond when she got really sick have been blown out of the water. I was going to be the attentive husband; understanding, caring, wise. I'd stroke her hair and say soothing things. I managed that for a while, but I can't even stand to be in the same room as her anymore.

I found myself standing over her as she slept this morning, wondering what I used to see in her. She lay there on her back, snoring with her mouth open, her hair stuck to her face. The room smelt of her; the stench of bedpans, sweat and farts. She looked nothing like the woman I married five years ago. Just the thought of touching her damp, scarred body fills me with revulsion. Every entrance to her body has become an inspection chamber for medical investigation. Endless ultrasounds should have produced pictures of our son kicking inside her like Wayne Rooney. All we saw were parasitic tumours eating our future.

I remember our wedding day, and how stunning she looked as she walked up the aisle towards me. I couldn't wait to be alone with her so I could get that dress off her and my hands on that incredible body. I wanted her so badly. I was amazed she'd have me, flattered that she loved me. Now I barely know her. Neither of us are the people we were then. We should have had the chance of a future; that was the deal. I didn't sign up for this.

Friday 17ᵗʰ February 2006

I'd just sat down for the first time today when I heard that fucking bell she uses. Naturally, I assumed there was an emergency: that's what it's there for. I ran upstairs to her bedroom and found her lying on her bed, all tearstained and blotchy.

'What's wrong?' I asked. I really was worried about her; she looked terrible. I should've known better.

'I need you!' she whimpered with an Oscar worth performance.

My jaw clenched so hard I could feel my pulse throbbing in my temple but I tried to keep my voice calm. 'So you're not in *pain*?'

She had the nerve to look hurt. 'Of course I am.'

'I'll go and get your painkillers then.' I was on my way out of the room when she called me back.

'They won't *help*, Spence.' Her soft voice jabbed at me through the semi-darkness. I could feel her continuous moaning and demands pressing in at me from all four walls. I did my best to stay calm, but I felt my nails digging into my palms. It was all I could do not to go across and slap her stupid little face.

'Well, what did you call me for if you don't want anything?' My throat was tight and the words were strangled.

She held her hand out to me and gestured that I should sit on the bed. I didn't move; I didn't trust myself to. After a moment she let her hand drop. 'Spence, I need to *talk* to you.' Her little voice pleaded.

'No you don't.' I told her. 'You've been talking to me all day.'

'You don't understand. Sweetheart, I don't have long left now and I need things to be ok between us. I want you to know I love you. It's going to be OK; I feel at peace.'

She didn't look at peace. Her face was contorted and stained red. As I stared at her words exploded out of me. '*Peace*? You're not at *peace*. What right have you got to feel at *peace*? You should feel guilty as hell. You feel at peace? Piss off!' I slammed the door and left her to it.

I shouldn't have said that. She's scared and I should be reassuring her but what can I say? I can hear that bloody bell again now. I can't go in there again tonight; I'll go mad if I do. I'll take her a nice breakfast in bed tomorrow.

Living with dying: and other clichés – Lorna's blog

January 7ᵗʰ 2006 09:06: Honesty day.

I've been building up to today for a long time. Spencer, my husband, was wonderful when I first received my diagnosis of stage three ovarian cancer. He's been there with me throughout, lending his support and chivvying me along. But now I've been told I've 'progressed' to stage four he's become distant. Sadly my progress doesn't warrant a gold star; apparently it means, *'there's nothing they can do'*. In effect, I'm dying. Trouble is, I received that diagnosis a good couple of weeks ago and Spencer still hasn't accepted it. His language hasn't even changed; he's still fantasising about distant futures with kids and homes in the country. I've had a hysterectomy for God's sake. The hardest thing is, every day since I've been diagnosed he's moved further and further away. I can't engage with him any more. All his talk is of 'fighting', 'not giving in' and 'winning the war'. He'll be up in front of the UN Security Council soon if he's not careful. This is his war on terror.

Every time I've tried to introduce some honesty into our conversations and talked about imminent futures with dying and funerals, he pulls away and goes and finds something practical to do. I can feel the cancer growing between us, pushing us apart. Truth is, I'm not sure whether that's because I'm going where he can't follow *(Death: the final frontier… to boldly go where no man can follow),* or whether it's due to our different takes on what's happening now. Both probably. Either way, I can't let things go on like this. I can't stand the thought of having to face death without him. I've weighed up what scares me most, the thought of this confrontation or dying alone and I've decided that the confrontation can't be put off any longer. That's why today is so important. It's showdown day. I'm going to confront him with my mortality (!)

_____

Sarah Hutchins

> *Hey Lorna, just read your post. You'll be fine. This is happening to you, not him, and it's time he accepted things on your terms. By the way, are you sure about the diagnosis? Doctors do get it wrong, and there are medical breakthroughs all the time. Don't give up hope!   7/01/2006 10:31*

Julie Dawkins

> *You go girl! Tell him how it is! He should be there for you. You get*
> *rid of him if he's no good!   7/01/2006 10:57*

January 7th 2006 22:36: Battle over?

Well, it's done. I'm glad I never entered the diplomatic services. What a disaster! For some reason, despite all the caring and considerate ways I'd rehearsed telling him, I decided to come out with it while he was standing over me holding a tray full of food. I launched into a speech about how I was passing away and the time had come to stop fighting and to accept I was terminal. What hideous metaphors! When did I become the woman who can't say she's dying? I think I might have even started off by saying something pathetic like 'Spence, I can't do this anymore.' In fact I know I did because he assumed that I meant I was bored and couldn't watch anymore TV!

In the end we had the inevitable row. You probably don't need me to write it down for you, I expect you heard him where you are. *I* managed not to shout though, so I can pat myself on the back and feel virtuous and ignore the fact that I no longer have enough energy to shout anyway.

In the end it turns out I completely misjudged everything. Our tiff hasn't cleared the air. In fact he stormed out of the room after he'd shouted at me and he hasn't been back since. And now I've been left even more resentful than before. I just want him to take me in his arms, stroke my hair and say *'Shhhh, don't worry, I understand. I'll look after you. Everything will be OK.'* Is that too much to ask? Instead he stood over me and shouted something like

> *'You want to die? You're going to give up on everything, just like*
> *that? After everything I've done for you you're going to give into*
> *the cancer? You're fucking pathetic. What was the point of any of*
> *this? You're on your own!'*

So I hope you'll excuse me if I slump off and feel sorry for myself. Sad thing is I feel even more alone than I did this morning.

I wonder if he does too.

Gemma Nicholas

> *You're not alone Lorna! You've got me! I'll listen to you whenever you want. Please email me! 08/01/2006 12:01*

Lucy Davies

> *Lorna, how can you say such terrible things? You're not horrible or irrational or pathetic. You have every right to feel sorry for yourself. Don't let him get to you. 08/01/2006 08:23*

January 23rd 2006 20:12: Lonesome tonight

I'm weakening fast. Hadn't really expected it to be this quick. Still got so much to sort out. It's in my bones now, so I only have a few weeks left. I knew it had to be something like that, it's felt different lately. Made the mistake of telling my doctor what was wrong (instead of letting him guess), which delayed the diagnosis. He did his *'now now, young lady'* voice and told me that the tests would have detected it if the cancer had spread. Keep forgetting that there is a way to tell doctors things – you must tell them the symptoms and let them feel like they've done all the hard work. It helps to follow up their diagnosis with wide eyes and a breathy statement like 'Oh doctor, I never thought of that. You're *so* clever!' It also has the benefit of you being regarded as a compliant patient. Very important, especially if you're not.

Dying is a lonely business. My parents come round occasionally to sit next to my bed and look stricken. They won't accept I'm dying either. Whenever I bring the subject up their eyes get even sadder and they say something like *'Well now, there's no good comes of that sort of talk. You need to think positive!'* in a brisk parental voice. I am *trying* to be positive but about death rather than the fiction they have constructed. Still, they never stay long, thank God.

Things aren't any better with Spencer. In fact they're worse. He avoids coming into the bedroom now unless he knows I'm asleep. I've got a bell to ring in case I need something, but he'll just dry up the spilt bedpan and leave me wet with tears. I wish he'd stop trying to fix everything and just sit with me a while. I need a husband not Bob the Carer (*Can he fix me? No he bloody well can't!*).

Pain is worse today. Mustn't tell doctor though or they'll put me on another drug with another side effect. Certainly won't tell them about the loneliness – there's probably an anti-loneliness happy pill new to the market that the doctor's been dying to try. I'm sure Spencer thinks I'm talking about dying because I'm depressed.

Susan Carr

> *Lorna, you're so brave. If anything like this ever happens to me, God forbid, I hope I'm half as brave as you. You are in my prayers.   23/01/2006 22:34*

February 17th 2006 18:21: End is nigh

It's close - can feel it. Ta for messages; they've been great comfort. Am less scared now. Tried to get Spence to talk to me but he won't. Thinks I just need to try harder. I love him so much and I hate him so much. He said I deserved to go to hell. Maybe I do.

Shouldn't be like this; should be peaceful; love and tenderness. 'Stead I'm alone. Know he'll feel guilty afterwards. Hope he does. P'raps I don't I mean that. All the stuff he did, but I just wanted him to listen. I don't want him to be unhappy. He must be happy. S'nothing to fear in death – it's dying that's hard. Keep ringing bell but he won't come. I miss him so much. He thinks it's him I'm leaving. It's him that's kept me going this long.

Fiona Marien

> *How dare he speak to you like that? You DO NOT deserve to go to hell. Sorry for shouting but you mustn't be thinking like this. Chin up! 18/01/2006 10:47*

Sarah Hutchins

> *Lorna, what's happening? Are you OK? Don't leave us in suspense like this. I'm worried about you. 20/01/2006 07:42*

Gemma Nicholas

> *Where are you? You really need to write a post. PLEASE! Not hearing from you is KILLING ME! PLEASE say you're OK.   20/01/2006 22:03*

Saturday 18th February 2006

I found her dead this morning. She died in the night. I went into her room with a tray full of her favourite things for breakfast. I'd even got her a flower. I pushed the door open with my foot and called out to her, but there was no reply.

'Good morning! Room service! I do hope you're not decent madam!' I hadn't gone many steps when the smell hit me. I've not been around death much before but it was the unmistakable stench of loss.

I dropped the tray and stood at the foot of her bed staring at her, trying to take in what I was seeing. She lay on her back, her mouth open and her eyes staring at the ceiling. The laptop lying next to her was still on. She looked like she'd been taken in the middle of the fight. I don't think she went willingly in the end.

I'm sat in the corner of her room now, waiting for the ambulance that will take her away. Someone, her mother I guess, has cut off the leg off a pair of tights and tied round her head to shut her mouth. There are two 2p pieces on her eyes. She doesn't look like my Lorna at all anymore.

I must ring the undertakers but I've told myself it'll wait. There are other things that won't, like spending these last moments alone with her. I could have spent last night with her in my arms. I could have held her and been held by her. I could have said sorry for all the ways I hurt her. How could she leave me with so much left unsaid? How could I have left so much unsaid? I want to go over there and shake her and shake her 'til she wakes up and I can say all the things I need to. I miss her so much my body aches. I can feel the bile rising in throat at the way I spoke to her, the hate I felt. My God I hope she doesn't know I felt like that. Did she know I loved her? My brain is numb at the thought of facing the rest of today without her, I can't even think about tomorrow without her.

Living with dying: and other clichés – Lorna's blog

March 19ᵗʰ 2006 02:06: Sad News.

Dear all,

Many of you have been following Lorna's blog since she started writing it soon after her terminal diagnosis. As you have no doubt guessed by now, Lorna (to use a phrase she would have hated) 'lost her battle' with cancer on 18ᵗʰ February 2006. She was 36.

Sadly she did not have time to write many entries on this blog. I was unaware of her writing, and only discovered it a few days before her funeral when I was using her laptop to find a reading. I'm sorry it's taken me so long to let you know about Lorna, I didn't know what to write. I would like to take this opportunity to thank you for the support you have given Lorna over her last months. Her diagnosis was the start of a very difficult time for her, and being able to share her story with you appears to have alleviated the loneliness she speaks of in her entries. Although it rips at me to know I caused her such sadness and isolation, it is a great comfort to hear her voice in her writing and to enjoy her sense of humour again. I hadn't given her much opportunity to express it lately.

I'm devastated that I made Lorna suffer towards the end. I'll never forgive myself for the pain I caused her. She showed so much more bravery than I was capable of. She was dignified to the last and deeply courageous in the face of death. Whilst reading Lorna's experience tears me to pieces, it has also made me very proud of her, even more so than before. She faced a situation where those she loved refused to let her speak, yet she spoke to you. When no one would listen she made herself heard.

I hope you might remember her now and then. Her inexplicable loss gains some meaning if you are inspired by her story and learn from my mistakes. I hope her story continues to touch lives after her death so that, in some small way, she can continue to live through her words.

Best wishes,

Spencer

Living without you

Gemma Pargeter

2nd February 1998

When I woke up this morning and pulled back the curtains to see the beautiful sight of freshly fallen snow, for a split second a smile spread across my face. Then I remembered. That was all it took. I spent the rest of the day in bed in a haze of tears and restless dreams. Dr Williams thinks it's normal and that I have to go through this 'stage' in order to move on, like writing this silly journal. It's not doing any good. I'm not going to move on. This is now my life, or more to the point, I don't have one. My life stopped on January 20th, when my husband's did.

14th February 1998

Ironic isn't it? Valentine's day has never meant much to me, I've always thought of it as a day for teenage crushes and courting couples. Yet today seemed wholly different; today I was alone and it was all too significant. I was supposed to be spending today with him. We should have been sipping our Chablis, giggling together at the Birch Hotel whilst we played our annual game of judging how long each couple had been dating and which poor soul had produced the most ridiculously lavish gift. Instead I was on an entirely different kind of date, my second in fact with a Dr Williams, my grievance counsellor.

20th February 1998

How can it have been a month? I can still smell his sweet musky cologne on his favourite red jumper. It often comes to bed with me to help me sleep but half the time it's hopeless, what starts as the comforting familiarity of his scent, turns into torment in the early hours of the morning as I reach to touch what is no longer there. Yet I can't bring myself to pack up his things, his life. My daughter Rebecca thinks it's not helping me by having his belongings around the house as though he were still here. She thinks by looking at them, it is a reminder that he's gone. Oh if only she could understand that I don't need a reminder of his absence, it's with me every waking minute of every day.

13th March 1998

Oh Robert, I can't do this anymore. I want to be with you, I need to be with you. How could you leave me all alone? It's so infuriating! Nobody understands…nobody knows what I'm going through without you. Oh, what am I saying? What's the use of this stupid journal?

28th March 1998

I just couldn't bring myself to celebrate yesterday. What's the use of growing another year older when you have nobody to share it with? I can't bear the thought of growing older and older, leaving my dear Robert behind, never ageing, never gaining another grey hair or wrinkle. It doesn't seem right. My Sarah told me to look on the bright side, that at least he lived to see two beautiful grandchildren. I know she means well, but that really doesn't help me right now. What about all the things he'll miss like finding Rebecca a nice husband and reaching retirement? Why should he miss these things? Why should I be grateful that he got to see some things and forget about all that he didn't see? There really is nothing to celebrate or be grateful for; Robert's gone and that's the end of it.

30th April 1998

When my eldest daughter, Rebecca, took control of the situation in a time when I couldn't and wasn't ready to, she booked me into these seemingly pointless sessions with Dr Williams to help me. I can't say if they are helping me, how exactly are they supposed to be helping me? Should I feel different? What am I expected to gain from our weekly appointments? Dr Williams, or Michael as he has asked me to call him (I've not managed to call him Michael yet, it seems a bit personal and unprofessional if you ask me), says it's up to me what I get out of our meetings. How absurd! I just want to be left alone. I'm only doing this to keep my children happy and prove to them that I'm perfectly capable of looking after myself. So far 'we' have established that I am not allowing myself to mourn and that this journal should help release my grievance in a positive fashion. To be frank, I struggle to understand how mourning can ever be positive.

17th May 1998

The garden's looking shabby at the moment. Sarah's Tom has offered to mow the lawn, which is rather sweet of him. Despite his shortcomings, Tom really has been a brick, and I think he's taken it upon himself to keep the house in order after the state I managed to get myself into over the gas bill last month. It's not fair, I shouldn't have to be paying the bills and fixing light bulbs, that was never part of the deal. How could you do this to me Robert? How could you leave me? You've taken the easy way out.

3rd June 1998

I can't face church anymore, all those pitying looks and worse than that are the knowledgeable answers of 'God chose him, he's in a better place'. Rubbish. Why take him away from me? We were so happy. How can there be a God? What about me? Does God care about leaving me alone, feeling as though my heart has been wrenched out, leaving a hole of nothingness in its place? Simple, there cannot be a God.

26th June 1998

Rebecca took me to one of her yoga classes yesterday to get me out of the house. We didn't talk much on the way there, then in the changing rooms she had so many people to catch up with and chatter away to that I went very much unnoticed. It helped to see Rebecca in the midst of friendship, to know that she has a supportive group of friends but I felt so cut off from everybody, like I'd forgotten how to interact. I ended up leaving the class early and catching the bus home. I just wasn't ready for that step.

22nd July 1998

Dr Williams says it's good to be angry, it's all part of the mourning process. I'm letting my feelings of grief escape. It's healthy for me. Well I can tell you it doesn't feel healthy. I hate the way Sarah winces when she sees me opening my mouth to speak, waiting for the next bitter sentence to part my lips. What an awful person I've become, I can't believe how wretched I feel. It's a vicious cycle, I know I'm being nasty so I try not to talk and then I'm resentful of the way Sarah doesn't come to visit as often as she used to and I end up snapping at her. She's looking tired. I think the twins are giving her trouble, they're not settling into nursery very well at all. It can't be easy for her, I understand she's lost her father too, but at least she has Tom. I think she sometimes forgets that by looking at how happy she is with Tom, it's a bitter reminder that I have lost the love of my life and nothing will ever replace that.

4th August 1998

Why did I let you leave the house? You told me you thought you had indigestion and I just let you go. I should have stopped you, made you sit down. It's my fault. Is that why I'm being punished now? It makes me so angry I don't know what to do with myself!

13th September 1998

Oh dear, I did it again yesterday; I went too far with Rebecca. Not only is she taking care of me but she's helping Sarah too. She's always been the same; the more reliable yet reserved one who always seemed to be in control. Even at the age of six she'd be there for Sarah who'd scramble into her bed in the middle of the night after a bad dream. She's so much like her father I find it unbearable to be around her sometimes. Rebecca is just so collected; she seems to handle things so well, far better than her emotional wreck of a mother. I know I channel my anger out onto her and it's not fair to her but she takes it so well and sometimes that in itself is enough to spur the anger in the first place.

15th October 1998

'Myocardial infarction', why can't they just say heart attack? Why do doctors feel the need to overcomplicate matters when all they really want to do is sort people into boxes? Does it make them feel superior to the rest of us if they think we can't understand what they're talking about? Or is it supposed to make us feel better if the problem is generalised by category? Mind you, I couldn't bear to re-live that experience and read about the pain he went through. Perhaps a medical term is better, more detached. Yet I don't see how he could have suffered from 'Coronary Heart Disease', when he was a perfectly healthy man. 'Disease' happens to those people who are permanently ill and can no longer live a normal life, not my darling Robert who was young, fit and healthy. It just doesn't make sense.

22nd November 1998

Happy Birthday darling.

30th December 1998

Christmas, what a nightmare! Sarah insisted that I go Christmas shopping with her as I'd not managed to set foot near the shopping centre with all those busy bodies rushing around with such purpose. I suppose she was right, what would I have done if I'd not managed to get the twins anything. On Christmas day, Rebecca picked me up and whisked me away to Sarah's on her way out of town to visit friends. I really just wanted to be left alone to sit in front of the television with a bottle of wine and let the day pass in peace but Rebecca is as stubborn as her father and wasn't hearing any of it, she believed the best thing for me was to be around family and keep myself busy. The twins loved their present and seemed to be as hyperactive and energized as ever as though nothing were wrong. But it was all wrong. That night Sarah and I held each other as we sobbed for you, for our Christmas, as we knew it. It will never be the same.

16th February 1999

I went to our library today and decided to take Michael's advice and have a little search on the Internet. Oh you should have seen me, it would have made you roar with laughter. I didn't even know how to turn the blasted machine on! The button was in a completely different place to our friendly companion at home. Thankfully Julia's boy was there on work experience (poor thing, those crazy old dears will eat him for breakfast). He was very good and talked me through it, step by step. I finally understand the term 'Google-it'! So I had a search and found sites full of people sharing their feelings and experiences, most of which are over expressive Americans. However I did find one rather warming site written by a lady younger than myself who only lost her partner three months ago and already seems to be coping far better than I ever could. I'm not sure I want to move on. I'm afraid of doing it on my own, birthdays, weddings, and Christmases without you. It's not how we planned it at all.

28th March 1999

Another year older, another year wiser (well I don't know about that last bit but I certainly feel older). Feeling older has absolutely nothing to do with the trying hangover I'm sporting today I'm sure! I was all ready to spend yesterday in my pyjamas with a good book and a pot of tea but my beastly daughters had other plans for me. Oh, it was so sweet of them. Rebecca had taken the day off work and Sarah's friend was watching over the twins. They had the whole day planned and were promptly banging at my door at eight in the morning to get started. We headed down to Brighton to have tea and scones in the Grand Hotel then spent most of the day shopping for the perfect outfit to wear that evening, although I had no idea what we were to be doing. It turned out to be a trip to the Theatre Royal then back to Rebecca's to finish off the day with a bottle of champagne. I'd not seen Rebecca and Sarah this close for such a long time, that it brought tears to my eyes (with the help of the champagne of course). I only wish you'd been there to see it.

2nd April 1999

What an emotional day I've had! Oh Robert, I found it. Tom must have knocked it off of your shelf when we were clearing clothes last week. It had fallen into the shoebox filled with holiday photos at the bottom of the cupboard. As I hauled the box out to sort through some things, I noticed it jutting out from behind the bright smiles of our beautiful girls grinning proudly in front of a sandcastle. I didn't know what it was at first, the little box looked so plain I would have discarded it, but then I noticed the red envelope with 'FEB 14th' stencilled on it. The feeling I felt was so strong, it was as though you were standing over my shoulder; your presence was so real that I felt an overwhelming sense of calm and relief.

'TO MY DEAREST ROSE, I LOVE YOU MORE THAN YOU COULD EVER IMAGINE.'

You have no idea how much I will treasure those words, that piece of you. My earrings are beautiful I'm almost afraid to wear them for fear I might lose one but I know how you feel about me hoarding my jewels so I promise you I will wear them as often as I can and know that you're with me every step of the way.

13th August 1999

Tom has been looking through my finances with me and it looks as though I'm going to have to start work again. It's a terrifying thought; I've not worked since the girls were born. Whatever will I do?

19th October 1999

My dear Rebecca, what an angel. She's been a fantastic help with this job-hunting business and practically rewrote my shabby old curriculum vitae for me and at last success! It's not a big responsibility but I'll be working four days a week as a receptionist in the Parkview clinic. It was Michael who put in the recommendation for me and with Rebecca's help I managed to persuade them that I was the right lady for the job!

3rd March 2000

You wouldn't believe how busy I've been my love. I've begun my own little widow's (yes, it means I have to say that word aloud now) group. We get together once a month and find some lovely new place to have lunch. Yesterday was my turn so I took them to that gorgeous pub at the end of

Slugwash Lane with the open range fire. Remember how we used to visit it on Sundays with our papers and sit on that big leather sofa sharing anecdotes from one another's amusing articles? Well I think the girls really enjoyed it and it was the first time Janet came out with us. She's doing much better this last month and has even agreed to meet Michael for a few sessions, which I know will help.

24th December 2000

Rebecca has agreed to bring her new man along to Sarah's for Christmas day so that we can all meet him. His name is James and apparently he's doing very well for himself and runs his own public relations company in Brighton. Things must be going very well between them for Rebecca to allow us to meet him. Oh, I just hope it works out and that she doesn't push him away. If only she could open herself up a little more and let people in, she has such a big heart, it would be impossible for anybody not to fall in love with her.

10th April 2001

Sarah called last night and wants everybody to go to hers for dinner tonight. It's such short notice, I hope everything's all right. Rebecca and James are picking me up any minute, but I just can't relax. I hope everything's OK with Tom's new job.

22nd November 2001

6lb 7oz! Sarah gave birth to a beautifully healthy baby boy at six o'clock this morning and with my blessing has decided to name him Robert. This day will always be your day but you now have a very special little grandson to share it with. What a gorgeous crisp sunny day it is too. I'm heading back to the hospital in a minute as Tom has just called to say Sarah and baby are both awake and well, so I'm off to get my first cuddle with my new grandson.

5th May 2002

Rebecca and James announced their engagement this evening. I must be the soppiest mother ever, I actually cried at the dinner table! I know she must be happy because her whole aura has changed; she's still reserved but now she's happy to hug her old mum and spend more time with the family. Her friendship circle is as large as ever (I can't even bear to think about numbers for the wedding!) but she seems to need them less these days and need James a little more. Sound familiar?

23rd June 2003

Dear Robert, I miss you terribly, but I'm doing OK. Love you forever, your Rose xxx

Communication

Anna Robottom

For the first time in months I feel calm, almost happy, as I set off to work, feeling like I could enjoy the day, that I should enjoy the day without worrying about Nikki. I remember the day I first found out she was ill; God knows how she managed to tell me. It must have been so awful for her, but it was such a shock to me that I just wasn't there for her at all. I had no idea what I should say to her. All she'd wanted at that moment was my reassurance and I couldn't even give her that. I felt so selfish, but still the only thoughts I could manage were wondering why it had had to happen to *my* best friend, *my* housemate and how unfair life was to me. As long as I can remember Nikki's been the one to look after me, reassure me when I've been scared and comfort me when things have gone wrong. She's been there through all the good times in my life as well, like when I finally plucked up the courage to tell our other housemate John how I really felt about him. That took months of her nagging - it must have been so frustrating for her living with the two of us, seeing all the signs but not being able to convince us they were there until we finally worked it out for ourselves. If I hadn't have had John there to hold on to I don't know how I would have coped the day Nikki went back home to her Mum, needing the support we just couldn't give her. And God knows I've felt guilty for not giving her enough of it since the start of her illness, but at least she knows how I feel, how much I love her.

Anyway, I don't know if it's the weather, the fact that I managed to get a good few hours sleep last night for the first time this month, or the fact that I have plans for tonight with all my friends, but I actually find myself smiling as I type in the security code to the entrance of the nursing home where I work. I take my time getting ready at my locker, checking the little details of my uniform; enjoying the precise image it's my job to project whilst inside the home. Hair pulled back into a neat bun, nametag clipped to my pocket, all those little things I do every day almost mindlessly but appreciate today. Upstairs, I pause as usual by the office, listening in on the phone call someone is always making, whether it is to another floor, a friend or relative, doctor or hospital, or even last week's entertainer, angry because he hasn't been sent the cheque he was promised. The internal calls are the most interesting, just because they so often turn out to be someone in trouble over one thing or the other. Also, overhearing these calls can often be the only way of finding things out about the residents; no one communicates properly here, that's the problem. Today it's Kris, one of the nurses dialling and I slow down almost absent-mindedly as I go past the desk, half interested in what she has to say, half delaying the moment when I actually have to start working. Motivation is never easy when you start work at half seven in the morning.

'…and you heard about the peg in room eight did you?

… Yeah, seven this morning, found her when they went in to get her dressed.

… Mmm

… Who what, found her? Oh, Claire -

…I know, poor thing, that's her second in two weeks; it'll be putting her off the night shift at this rate!

… I'm just about to phone them, we'll need her stuff shifting by the end of the week, there's an assessment at St James' needs the bed.'

It takes me a minute to realise it's Annie they're talking about. Christ, poor bugger. Only seventy five and still plenty of stories to tell, when there's some in here that have been on death's door for months. They lie there, hardly able to talk and yet they just keep on going, keep on taking one last gasp of breath after you think they must have taken their last. I really like Annie – suppose that's liked now, funny how often in this job we have to start using past tense so suddenly and just accept it as routine. They say these things get easier the more often you go through them, well I've been working here three years now and I can't feel it getting any better. I do manage to leave most of it behind at the end of the day, but that's about as far as any sign of it getting easier goes. Problem is, no matter how upset you are it doesn't do to show it; there are other residents to consider and it can't be good for them to fret. I suppose it must be quite a worry for them really, constantly seeing people the same age as them going so regularly. If it was me I'd be wondering when it was going to be my turn, after all, by the time you get to that age you've got to be expecting it haven't you? Not like when it's someone young. Not like Nikki. Not that she's going to die, I know she'll be fine in the end, but just suppose. Now that would be a whole different story, a tragedy. I don't know how I'd manage. Unlike here, now, when we have no option but to cope. Working in a place like this you have no choice other than to get on with the day, but ready to be understanding and sympathetic should any grieving relatives come to visit. I go into Annie's room to take a last look as I walk past, and bump into Katy who seems to have had the same idea. I suppose it's our way of saying a little good bye so that we can move on and care for whoever comes along to take their place. And there will be a new lady in her bed by next week, especially if Kris is on the case already, but then, I suppose that's business. Empty beds just don't pay. It's just a bit weird when its Annie's room one week, someone else's the next. They change so often, so fast.

'It's a shame, isn't it? It always seems to be the sweet ones that go first.'

I smile in reply, an understanding between the two of us of how little we can let ourselves feel sad. There's always that urge to lighten the mood, to try and find a memory that will somehow justify the death; one that's somehow always cute or funny - the funny ones are the best. It seems to make it easier to deal with losing a favourite resident if we let ourselves focus on the amusing memories we have of them, rather than the sad ones. I don't know why, perhaps it kind of trivialises the situation, but in a good way.

'Do you remember that time when' – see what I mean – 'she threatened to ring the police because she thought poor little Dorothy had stolen her best nightie?'

We both laugh, though I have a sneaking suspicion that actually it wasn't Annie who had raised the alarm over a nightie but Florence; the time Annie threatened to phone the police was when her slippers were in the wash and she wouldn't leave her bedroom without them. That sort of thing happens surprisingly often in here, but it still makes you laugh. Actually, I suppose working in a home like this would be a whole lot more difficult if you couldn't laugh at some of the stuff that goes on. It's helped anyway, and we carry on down the corridor; time to get on with the day, and with everyone else's lives.

The shift goes relatively quickly, as it always does when you work mornings. There's just so much to get done – breakfasts to give out, beds to make, baths to give, tea to pour, lunch to serve, always something else to keep you busy. And that seems to be what I need most at the moment. There's a strange mood in the air all day long, a respectful quiet in the staff room over compensated for by loud, bubbly exchanges with the residents. Annie's family come in after lunch, and we offer our condolences, noting as we do that the family doesn't actually seem to be in much need of consolation.

'Of course, we'd been expecting it for a while now, it makes it easier.'

Yeah right, try telling that to Nikki's mum and dad. It's nearly a year now since they found out that their baby girl could be dying, but it's still far too much for them to accept. Her mum's managed to distract herself with looking after Nikki, on the go none stop, but God knows what she'll do if… not that she can die of course, not my best friend. She's too strong to give up.

The fact that the last time anyone saw Annie's niece in the building was last Christmas Eve doesn't really prompt the highest level of sympathy anyway. Annie always said it was us that made her smile each morning, not them. What's the point of family if they're never around? Not that my mum's around much, but at least I've got Nikki and John there for me. I think when it comes down to it, it's those people who come through for you when you need it most that are your real family. Annie's family didn't mean anything to her by the end, and I don't think she meant much to them either, which is sad as I reckon she'd make, or have made, sorry, a lovely grandma, the kind that spoils you and says embarrassing things but you love all the same. The kind of grandma I'd have given anything to have. Except she did mean one thing to them – on their way out Katy hears them talking about the will, and its clear they only came in to make sure there wasn't a penny left behind. Money, that's always the thing they're interested in. It makes you sick.

I find myself actually quite relieved to be leaving work at the end of my shift, funny that I felt so bright about going there this morning. I suppose that's part and parcel of the job though; you never know what you might have to deal with in any one day. Anyway, at least I can push it out of my head as I walk down the road, and forget about it until tomorrow. For now I'm thinking about me, and only me. And Nikki of course, but that goes without saying; she's my best friend and I don't know what I'd do without her. It's still early enough for the sky to be blue, yet there's a crisp autumnal chill that clears my head, and I take a minute to just enjoy breathing. Until you've worked in the heat of a nursing home I'm sure you can never fully appreciate the sudden shiver of stepping outside into the cold, sharp air. Of course, the thought of John waiting for me at home makes me appreciate the feeling even more; there's nothing like the anticipation of coming in from the cold straight into someone's waiting arms. And those arms have given me so much comfort these last few months, they've kept me going, filled the gap where I used to turn to Nikki but no longer feel that I can. It wouldn't be fair to burden her now that she's already going through so much herself. John says it might be a welcome distraction for her but I'm not so sure.

I pause at the playground where I used to stop sometimes on my way home from school, and sit down on the swings. The familiar, gentle rocking has a soothing effect on me, a physical lullaby. I find it's a good way to clear my head after a hard day at the home; a good way to empty it of all work related thoughts and refill it with me. I remember playing on these swings with Nikki when we were little, talking about all the exciting adventures we'd go on when we grew up, what exotic holidays we'd take, how we'd make the world a better place, cure cancer – oh the ironies of childhood dreams! – and, of course, arguing over who could swing the highest. It was always Nikki who got highest which I knew perfectly well but would never admit to; she seemed to have all the luck back then. Well, I suppose it couldn't last, life's not like that. One time I fell off the swing and it was Nikki that took me back home to my mum, Nikki who told me not to cry, that I'd be all right. Two years later, after a fight with my mum it was her that I ran to for comfort. She hid me in her room until her dad found me later that evening and drove me home, but not before we'd made a pact that as soon as we were old enough we'd live together, we'd look out for each other, look after each other.

All my life Nikki's been telling me I'll be all right, how come I find it so hard to say the same to her now that she needs the comforting and not me? Why do I long for her to reassure me, to tell me that everything's going to be O.K. when it's her that's going through all this, when I know how scared she is? I look for the words every day, but they never come. For the tenth time today I picture the moment she told me about the cancer, she looked so scared, and I just thought, why *my* friend? It just didn't seem fair. I was only twenty-one; far too young to lose my best friend, it just didn't seem fair. I cry, and am soothed by the steady motion of the swing, feeling my breathing slowly clear until I feel like I can cope again, until life seems manageable once more. I am filled with a new sense of calm determination that I can be strong, I have my friends, my boyfriend, my job - there's no reason why I can't be there for Nikki when all those people are there for me every day.

Gradually I start to feel like I can actually handle things by myself, that I can be a good friend to Nikki again. I decide to go and visit her in the morning and actually talk about what *she* wants, not what I feel like I can cope with hearing. I think I'll arm myself with a few gossip magazines, some chocolate and an apology, and hopefully we can just get back to how we were before she got ill. The last time I saw her she never mentioned the way I've been distancing myself, but if I'm honest I could see that's what she was thinking. I'm sure she knows how much I love her but tomorrow I think I'll tell her anyway, just to remind her. It's always nice to hear that someone loves you, and I'm sure it'll make me feel a lot better too to know that I've said it. When we see people get ill at work it always seems so much sadder if they have nobody there that they know or trust; they must be so much more scared. Of course Nikki has her friends and family, but from now on I'm going to do my best to make her feel as loved and supported as possible.

Walking home I smile again, looking forward to seeing Nikki and thinking about my plans for the night. I know John's cooked for me and then we're going out with our new housemate, Helen and some old friends we still know from school. It's ages since I've been out with all my old mates; that's the problem with shift work. I know there's a reason why we haven't kept in touch more efficiently but it's still nice to see the same old faces every now and then. This past year it's seemed like every time they all go out for a good time I'm stuck at work, caring for old, sick people, half of whom can't even remember my name. Not that I mind, really, it's just that I don't want to feel old before my time. We should make the most of being young, you never know what's round the corner - Nikki's proved that. So I've decided I'm going to have a really good night tonight, nothings going to get in my way.

Going in through the door I know at once that I'm wrong. John is stood waiting for me and one look at his face is enough to tell me what I somehow already know, the real reason I felt calm on the swings, felt different walking home. And yet, as I hear the words I can't believe they could be true, can't see John's expression anymore through the stream of tears running down his face, down my face. It's not fair. Young people don't die, my friends don't die, Nikki can't die. I never said goodbye.

Extinguished

Hayley Smith

Everything can look shiny from the outside. It's when it comes to examining the inside that the light recedes and failures seep out of the darkness. Apparently what I had was enviable and I suppose it was but at the same time, it was superficial. I was an unmitigated material girl. I worked my arse off to get everything I wanted and thought I could do anything. I followed the common proverb 'everything can be achieved if you set your mind to it'. Yeah right. Whoever came up with that one didn't account for the unpredictable nature of my body. The one thing I had absolutely no control over. It was a darkness that started as a shadow and grew into a full-blown black hole. A black hole that got larger and sucked up my life and everyone else in it.

I had had a plan when I was little that I would get a fantastic job, get married when I was 26 and have children at 32. A simple plan that I really didn't stick to. I'd been propelled through life at an incredible speed and I suppose I got carried away with the 'fantastic job'. Mark and I thought we had plenty of time to have kids. That was a mistake. The irony of it was that I had been pregnant before when I was 20. It was an accident. It happened so easily; I thought it would be just as easy to get pregnant again. I didn't want kids then. The decision to keep it wasn't really an option. I was having fun, enjoying being young and single. Possibly enjoying it a bit too much but it was all just a laugh and it was definitely not the right time or situation to bring a kid into. I don't have any regrets except that I didn't try to get pregnant again earlier. When I did decide it was about time to have kids it wasn't physically possible. It wasn't for the lack of trying. Not to start with anyways. Great, spontaneous sex turned into a passionless chore as Mark's interest waned and every month presented yet another failed attempt. The IVF gave us the option of succeeding where nature couldn't.

The smell of disinfectant was overpowering at first and I was engulfed by it. In a peculiar way it became the essence of why I was there. It was hope and disappointment entwined. I figured IVF was worth the intrusion. I was there for one reason; we were all there for one reason. At least I wasn't on my own in there. I didn't have to hide my failures because we were all in the same boat and we were all asking for help. I thought I was the only woman to go through this but all the couples sitting in that waiting room made me realise I wasn't the only unlucky one. I was however, the only one to be sitting in there on my own, without the support I so desperately needed.

It took over an hour to be called through by the doctor. He was 'talking me through' the procedure but the overload of information was too much. I was still stuck on his first words. 'Rhiannon, you have to realise only 21.8% of In Vitro Fertilization treatment cycles result in a birth. It is important that you realise that IVF fails more often than it succeeds.' I wasn't exactly filled with confidence. I heard him going on about 'gonadotrophin drugs' and 'human chorionic gonadotrophin' but he could have been going on about anything. How the hell was I supposed to know what he was talking about? He wasn't 'talking me through' the procedure; he was just reeling off his medical knowledge. Making himself sound intelligent and leaving me in a complete daze. He was like a tape, just repeating himself over and over again to different couples. No doubt the couple that went in after me heard exactly the same speech.

Two years before we decided on the IVF, we thought there was a chance that I was pregnant. I had waited so long to see that blue line appear but those three minutes of waiting seemed to be the longest. 'Is it ready yet?' Mark was acting like a child, but he wasn't the only one that couldn't wait. 'It's not going to happen any quicker if you keep asking.' I was talking through the door to him because I couldn't deal with the look of disappointment. That time was different though. He didn't even ask if it was positive. I handed him the pregnancy test and an ecstatic smile pasted itself across his face. That smile didn't leave his face for weeks. Every other day he was coming home with presents for the baby and me. It was too early to know the sex but he was buying all the clothes in white and yellow just to be on the safe side; although a miniature ManU football shirt managed to work its way into the pile of baby clothes. We put all the clothes in a box in the attic after I lost it. I was only pregnant for 5 weeks. It was as though my body realised how happy I was and decided I didn't deserve it.

The actual IVF treatment just seemed to be at the end of a long list of tests and questions. The initial tests didn't show anything. Apparently we were both fertile, producing the right stuff. It was just unexplainable infertility. Typical. It was suggested that I go for an ultrasound to check everything was where it should be. I couldn't see how anything had moved since last time, but figured I should humour the medical professionals and desperation is a powerful thing. I had hoped that despite the fertility clinics, we would have miraculously conceived and be well on our way to a baby, but the realisation had fallen like a coffin lid.

The gel was freezing cold which didn't help the fact that I was dying for the loo. They wanted a full bladder so that's what I gave them. But I definitely regretted my smugness. Combined with the pressure from the ultrasound, I was desperately trying to hold it in by distracting myself and keeping my mind off running water. The blind on the window of the door was crooked. It was one of those metal ones with the slats that bend just by knocking it slightly. It looked cheap, but I suppose it was only there to serve one purpose and keep prying eyes out. It was not as though it had to look pretty. I was bought back to reality by the gynaecologist. 'There appears to be a cyst in your ovary'. I couldn't figure out if he was being serious or just trying to stop me looking at the cheap blind. He kept running the ultrasound over the same area of my stomach, appearing quite concerned. I was so focused on getting pregnant that I didn't quite comprehend what he was implying. 'Will it affect my chances of getting pregnant?' I must have had the most moronic look on my face, a naïve, bewildered look that caused his blunt and vaguely bitchy response. 'I don't think you quite understand. It shows solid areas, which are potentially cancerous. You need a blood test and needle aspiration to determine whether it's just a cyst or ovarian cancer '. I felt winded; there was nothing I could say. My pathetic body just seemed to be spiting me. One thing after another.

'The blood test detected CA125. It's a chemical given off by cancer cells. We use it as a tumour marker. The biopsy confirmed it.' I didn't want the medical rubbish. I needed it in layman's terms. The doctor didn't seem to give a shit that there was a person behind the cancer. They talked at me rather than to me, expecting me to know what they were talking about. The oncologist gave me my so-called options, which were brief to say the least. It all seemed to be dependant on what they called the cancer's 'personality features'. Why did it have to sound like it was living? It had invaded my body and then been given a 'personality'. I felt absolutely useless. Mark was desperately trying to be supportive but didn't have a clue. How could he? According to him the doctors were just 'trying to help' but that was all very well because it wasn't happening to him. It wasn't his insides that they wanted to chop up. Why had my career had to take priority? Maybe if I'd given my first baby the chance, then my body wouldn't hate me. At least it might have reduced the risk.

Sod's bloody law. The doctors insisted on doing tests before the operation to remove the cancer. The number of pregnancy tests I had taken made me immune to the results. Mark and I had hardly been trying and the cancer had more or less destroyed my sex drive. I was called in to the hospital for what I thought was another blood test or discussion about the stage of my cancer, but when I got there the doctor's face seemed to be full of pity.

I had finally got what I wanted. I was pregnant and the only thing between my baby and me was the life-sucking lump.

Why is it called being under the knife? As if it isn't scary enough as it is. It felt as though I'd had a few glasses of wine. Actually it felt as though I'd had a few bottles. I was trying to keep myself awake but the general anaesthetic overrode my every emotion and anxiety.

'Rhiannon?' It was like a hangover, the morning after the very heavy night before. I felt like shit and probably looked just as bad. 'I'm so sorry Rhiannon.' It was one of two things and I didn't want to hear bad news about either of them. Why did I have to wake up? I didn't know which would be worse, losing my baby with the slim chance of beating cancer or having my baby and not living long enough to see it grow up. Like I said, sod's bloody law. I thought I had all the power in the world to achieve what I wanted but it obviously wasn't the case. There was no screwing with my body. It had made its own decisions and there was nothing I could do.

'Rhiannon, the cancer was too advanced. It spread to your fallopian tubes and your womb. We can remove it all but you're going to need a full hysterectomy and chemotherapy. I'm afraid your baby won't survive.' The black hole might have receded back into a shadow, but it had succeeded in taking away a precious life and any future hope.

Things can look shiny from the outside. Sometimes they are and sometimes they just aren't meant to be.

Part Three: Difference

Beans or tomatoes?

Arran O'Kane

I stood under the florescent cafeteria light, pressing my stomach against the warmth of the steel hot plate, starring at the identical empty sterile tables. I pushed my tummy further up against the hot metal, rubbing my hands together over the steam, enjoying the warmth that would later make me sweat. The large tobacco stained clock read just before 9.05 am, I'd barely been there five minutes. I quickly vowed not to look at the clock for the rest of the day.

The place was empty and usually stayed that way until just after ten, when the first huddle of bleary eyed, sallow skinned suits trudged in. Meetings both began and finished on the hour, every hour, so the majority of people appeared at the counter between the hour and ten minutes past. The remainder of the hour consisted of maintenance workers, stomping over to the counter in their leather boots and neon Velcro jackets. I would watch them grab the counter with both hands, dry and creased, already grime having worked its way under their fingernails. They would lean on the counter, leering at us and licking their lips, not only salivating over the bacon.

I had worked with Cam for four weeks. She'd started at the canteen a week after me, although you wouldn't know it because she'd caught on far quicker. On her fourth day she stopped listening to Robby, the stuttering kitchen hand, I still found myself lugging the stinking rubbish bags outside when he asked me to. Cam was no fool. After a week, she had started flirting outrageously with the maintenance workers, regardless of their grimy fingernails.

Her full name was Camila, but she was far more of a Cam than a Milly. In contrast to me, she was small and athletically built. She flew round the canteen like a machine, never pausing to gaze at the clock or simply into thin air, which I constantly found myself doing. Her hair was the colour of tomato soup and after a day standing over a hot plate and a deep fat fryer, her fringe stuck to her forehead.

I was about to embark on my third week in the Moon & Richardson canteen. I'd taken the job after I realised that I couldn't stay at home in peace anymore. My step-dad Ian had reappeared and was doing my head in. Ian was disgusting and I'm not saying that just because he's my step-dad, my real dad is possibly even worse. Ian used to be a baggage handler at the airport and he doesn't let us forget it. He lost his job in cutbacks or something and hasn't been back to work since. But anyway, the point is that when he is staying with us (which is when HE pleases) he generally just stomps around the house glaring at me.

So I decided to get a job. One of my mum's mates said that Moon & Richardson were looking for staff. I went for an interview and the next week found myself in the greasy canteen with everyone else. To be honest, I wasn't sure what the company did, although I thought it was something to do with advertising. But I soon found out that it didn't really matter as far as I was concerned, my job was to put the rancid food on the plates.
I started at nine in the morning. We dished out sausages and eggs with beans or tomatoes until twelve and then we did lunch, dishing out more mass-produced food until four and then we would clean up.

After the first two days of this, I seriously began to think a day with Ian might be preferable. But then I got paid. I forgot how great having a pay check can be. After months of nothing you've suddenly got just over a hundred quid to play with. Obviously my Mum took the first big lump for money she said I owed her in rent and she really isn't worth arguing with sometimes. I suppose I am nineteen now and she really doesn't have to let me live with her anymore, if Ian had his way I wouldn't.

But anyway, yesterday was my second payday and I had some money to spend! Finding ourselves in the same position, Cam and I decided to take the bus into town. I always have a change of clothes in my rucksack: I like to wear my uniform for as little time as possible. We managed to change out of our stinking uniforms in the foot well of the backseat.

Cam is from in town; I live on the outskirts, one day I'd quite like to move in town, there's more stuff to do. It's boring where I am and I hate it, everyone knows each other and it makes me sick. I can't do anything without my mum or Ian finding out and of course everyone knows all about our situation. Some of Mum's mates have stopped talking to her again now Ian's back. She's so stubborn sometimes, she knows I hate him and that some of her best friends don't like him, but she just doesn't listen and she pretends she doesn't give a toss. I see her through my window in the morning waiting for the bus with all her work friends, standing in their uniforms, puffing on their cigarettes and she just talks to them like it hasn't happened. Like it isn't blindingly obvious that he's split her lip again.

*   *   *

Anyway, Cam and I made our way into town, amongst all the old ladies on the bus in their rain bonnets. I was so desperate for a fag that I had to ask Cam for one, I make an effort not to take cigarettes off people, like Ian takes them from my Mum, I'd rather buy my own. Cam pulled out a packet of Camel's; I chuckled, 'Where d'you get them from?' I asked as she offered me the pack.

'Got them off my Dad, he's just got back from holiday, got a load cheap at the airport.' 'Wicked.' I replied, wanting to stub my cigarette out on Ian's arm for never doing the same.

He and my Mum have only been on holiday once and that wasn't even abroad, they went to Brighton to stay with his mate Darren and she ended up coming back without him anyway.

* * *

Cam and I decided to go for a drink, seeing as it was a Friday. I've never really been much into drinking, smoking is far better. When I was at school I used to hang around with a bunch of mates and we'd sit outside the shop drinking cider and smoking. I can't remember the amount of times I was sick behind the wheelie bins outside the shop, but definitely too many. Those were the years when I guess I was happiest though, just drinking and smoking, out of the house all night and at school during the day.

I'd been at work all greasy and sweaty, having suits speak to me like I was an idiot all-day. And the thought of going back to the flat to find Ian wasn't exactly appealing either, so Cam and I sat and had a couple. I don't drink cider anymore, too old for that now; I drink gin and tonic like my Mum.

I noticed all the guys in the pub were turning their heads our way, slowly dragging their eyes over my greasy hair and lanky body and settling them on Cam, who had slipped into quite a low top whilst on the bus. Maybe it was because I hadn't had a drink in quite a while, or perhaps because I hadn't eaten all day but that gin and tonic hit me. Making me dizzy and relaxed, I suddenly felt far better than I had in a long time. We had a few more and Cam said she had to go to meet her boyfriend.

By the time I got on the bus home I was starting to feel a bit queasy and as I opened the front door to our semi it turned to nausea. The mirror in the hallway was smashed; the tiny shards of light were twinkling in my face.

'Mum?' No answer. I carried on through to the living room, broken furniture but no sign of her. Where was she, my stomach did a summersault, turning the gin over and over.

I found her in the kitchen sitting balled up on the floor by the washing machine, her face in her hands. I crouched down next to her wrapped my spidery arms around her withered frame. I buried my head in her shoulder smelling the sweet mixture of soap and fag smoke.

'You're bleeding Mum.' I said, noticing the trickle of blood from her nose and lips. It was fucking Ian; I didn't have to say anything, we both knew.

'Mum he's not coming back again this time, please.' Again she didn't reply she just sobbed softly into her hands.

All that happened last Friday and Ian hasn't been anywhere near the house since. So on Monday morning, as I stood in Moon & Richardson warming my stomach on the hot plate and noticed him walk in, I wasn't prepared. There was no way I was expecting to see his belly bulging out of his fluorescent jacket, the dirt under his fingernails, joking with the other maintenance guys. He must have got a new job I thought. I started to sweat and managed to scold the skin between my t-shirt and trousers on the hot plate. I stood there frozen, as Cam sauntered up to them and giggled at something he said. I watched him slowly make his way down the hot plate, helping himself to countless soggy sausages and oily eggs, finally he got to me, smiling.

'Beans or tomatoes?' I asked.

*   *   *

Within days Ian was back with my Mum again. I came home one evening to find his ample body spread over the sofa, a warm can of Stella in one hand and one of Mum's fags in the other. He said nothing to me, just smirked and carried on watching Eastenders. I went to find Mum in the kitchen, after what happened at the weekend she had promised me he wouldn't be coming back again.

'Mum. What's going on?' I asked, she kept her back to me whilst she did the washing up. 'What is he doing here?' I struggled to keep the disgust from my voice, but that's exactly how I felt, disgusted, everything about Ian sickened me.

'He's come back love.' She replied meekly. I couldn't stand to hear anymore, I know she didn't want to be pushed either so I walked straight out the front door again. I swallowed the lump in my throat as I walked down our soggy front path and through the gate onto the street. I decided to call Cam; she'd cheer me up for sure.

We arranged to meet in town; I caught a night bus and found her waiting for me at the bus park. Her hair was stuck to her head from the rain and her mascara had run under her eyes.

'Ah mate, you alright?' She grabbed me round the waist and gave me a squeeze; she couldn't quite reach my shoulders.

'Yeah I'm fine, I just need a drink.'

'Come on then.' She dragged me into town, to the pub we'd gone to a few days before.

'So was that your step-dad the other day? The new guy who came in with all the maintenance workers?' Cam asked me.

'He's got a new job working on the new building at Moon & Richardson and he's not my step-dad, my Mum isn't married to him.'

'Oh right, well I take it you aren't a fan of his then?'

'You could say that.' I took a gurgerly sip from my gin and tonic.

'Well I thought he looked like a twat if that makes any difference. They're all a bunch of dirty tossers those lot. Sleazy buggers, I only flirt with them cause I'm bored. Got to amuse myself somehow at work, nothing else to do.'

'How's the boyfriend' I asked, wanting to change the subject and I knew from past experience this was Cam's favourite.

'Oh him, we broke up last night, the dickhead reckons I'm cheating on him.'

'Are you?' I asked

'Not anymore, I'm not. Wish I was though, the amount of stick he's giving me about it, I might as well have.'

'Sod him then. If he doesn't realise what he's got then he's an idiot.'

'Awww mate.' Cam gave me a friendly push. 'So what are we going to do about this Ian bloke?'

'Shoot him.' I offered, she laughed.

'Only if you can get your hands on a gun.' I thought about the hunting gun that he keeps under his bed. He's such an idiot; he never even went hunting for God's sake. Just said he liked to have it just in case. I'd seen him taking pot shots at birds through the open bedroom window in his manky dressing gown.

'Have you spoken to your Mum about it?'

'Of course I have Cam, she just doesn't fucking listen. I reckon sometimes I'm even more angry with her for letting it happen to be honest.'

'Well I think you should try again, she's got to start listening to you sometime. My Mum never listens to me, but I've never really been in your situation, so it's not really the same.'

'Hmmmm. It's hopeless Cam. I'm thinking of moving out anyway, get out of the estate. I'm sick of it there.'

'Where you going to go?'

'See if I can get somewhere in town, I'll only have to work for another month, I've been saving up for a deposit.'

'That's wicked. But you're not going to leave work though are you? If you leave there's no way I'm staying there on my own. I'd be the youngest by

about forty years.'
'I dunno, Cam I hate it, it's shit.'
'You're right, it is shit, maybe we should both leave, but where else you going to work?'
'I dunno, hairdressing or something.' Cam let out a splutter and nearly knocked over her pint. When she'd recovered, she must have noticed the look of defeat on my face. She rubbed my arm,
'You'll be alright mate.' She sighed.

*   *   *

I decided to walk home and it took me ages but I was feeling pretty crappy to tell the truth. Talking to Cam had kind of made me realise how shit things actually were. As the bus pulled onto our street, I thought I could see a police car parked down our road under the fluorescent street lamps. It wasn't an unusual sight, they often drove round our estate but all the same I became worried, I was wary of the police. I made my way off the bus and as I got closer I realised, as well as the police car there was an ambulance and they were both outside my house. My stomach did a somersault and I felt the blood drain from my head, I started to run but my legs wobbled and shook. I thought I was going to be sick, please don't let him have killed her I thought, I couldn't bear the thought that Ian had finally gone too far. That idiot had finally really hurt my mum, maybe even killed her. I knew he was capable of it and she was too blind to stop it.
'Mum' I tried to scream but no sound came out, just a rasping kind of whisper. I banged on the front door and fumbled for my key; the house seemed empty. A policewoman opened the door and I almost fell into her. She was wearing her full gear, complete with a truncheon and a frown.
'Where's my Mum?' I managed to ask.
'Do you live here?' She had a deep voice and her breath smelt like stale smoke.
'Yes' she nodded and led me through into the sitting room, I noticed no furniture was overturned as I'd expected. A large male policeman sat on our beige sofa with a notebook and there, huddled in Ian's chair was Mum. I ran over to her and buried my head into her hair crispy with hairspray, she hugged me back. I looked over her shoulder and noticed Ian's hunting gun on the carpet by the dining table.
'What's going on?' I asked clinging to my Mum. 'Where's Ian?'

Mum and the police were all quiet. I scanned the room, most of the furniture looked normal. The gun lay abandoned on the floor and suddenly I realised, that ambulance hadn't been for Mum at all.

Betwixt: My Silent History –
A story of adoption

Lee Pinfold

Sitting alone in a corner of a darkened room, with nothing more than my imagination to keep me company, I prepare myself for another journey into and along the Information Superhighway:

Press flashing green button…. check!

Hard drive booting up………..check!

Power to monitor…………......check!

Icons fully loaded…….....…..check!

Internet access approved…….check!

Enthusiastically, I lift myself from the soft contours of my Herman Miller and, accompanied by the usual squelch of 'uncompounding' leather, I shuffle a little closer towards my desk. The radial glare emitted from the monitor – blinding amid such darkness (now there's a paradox) – creates an eerie, yet surprisingly comforting setting. In fact, I can see the attraction for those gullible moths, whose futile attempts of 'capturing the sun' keeps them occupied throughout long summer nights. However, tonight it is I and not those poor unsuspecting moths, who will attempt to capture some realisation of a far-removed certainty. Sitting upright with hands poised over the shadowy keyboard, I gingerly finger in the seven letters that form the word that has been restlessly playing on my mind:

Google Search - ADOPTEE

The results appear thick and fast: 983,000…in 0.32 seconds. 'Wow! There must be a lot of lonely people out there', me-thinks, whilst trying to comprehend the hodgepodge of information – all of which is competing to be my electronic chaperone: *Adoptee Birth-family Connections*; *Adoptee Searcher's Handbook*; *Adoptee's - Right to Know*; and even, *BASTARD*

NATION (American, of course!). My curiosity rubber stamped, I enter the domain of the *BASTARD NATION,* half expecting it to be a front for some 'teenage dirtbag' rock group whose mal-manufactured identify is reflected by their hormonal grievances. But of course I was wrong!

Alongside its mission statement to '…end a hidden legacy of shame, fear and venality', the site also features a publication entitled, 'Adopted Child Syndrome Family Cookbook: Ordinary Meals for Extraordinary Families' (???). After a little probing to try and find out exactly what pearls of wisdom, or even culinary delights this book has to offer (which alas evaded my puzzled mind), I stumble upon the *BASTARD NATION* online shop. The cookbook aside, also for sale (though for cultural reasons, I abstain from purchasing) are: *BASTARD* bumper stickers, *BASTARD* caps and, for the more discerning bastard – a *BASTARD* T-shirt. Reclining slowly, if not a little awkwardly, back into the comforts of Mr Miller, I digest my newfound bastard status and suddenly realise the irony – my biological father was American!

Although I have always known I was adopted and this is something that I'm grateful for, I was told only very little about my birthmother and nothing at all about my birthfather. Curiously though, I do remember my Mom (adoptive) telling me that as a small child I had an unusual fixation with the American flag. How true this was, I can't recall, though I suspect now that it was her way of letting me know something that I couldn't possibly have known at that time. That said, in its own paradoxical way – it worked – as I was to find out in the years to come.

Strangely, (but not uncommon – according to the many adoption devoted books that I have purchased recently) my experiences as an adoptee have run along similar paradoxes and tensions. One prime example and which seems to be common in adoption narratives, is the family gathering. Harmless in itself, such occasions however, inevitably turn to talk (gossip) of family history; familial likenesses in looks and habits; and talk of the usual genetic disorders, which most families seem to thrive on.

Similarly, Darren (my younger brother – not adopted) and I, accompanied by our two cousins – Dean and Jason, would be gathered at our Grandparent's terraced house on Brookmeadow lane each and every Saturday. Nan's terrace was a bundle of fascination for us all, sporting an array of knick-knacks from a bygone era. From hideously deformed cacti that sat mesmerising on the indoor windowsills (next to horrific school photographs of the four of us), to atomic era influenced furniture and objet d'art that sported a range of mutli-coloured balls, or *nodules*; the wonderful contents of Nan's house was enough to keep us four young prepubescent boys occupied and enthralled for hours on end. When not exploring the mysterious, and the exotic, or when we were all gathered together for a round of jam sarnies and a beaker of Ribena, we sat crossed legged in pairs in Nan's lounge, either side of the mustard-coloured tiled fireplace, listening to tales of a far removed yet tangible past. Whilst Granddad would always espouse the virtues of Socialism and the calamities of Aston Villa, the matriarchal powers that be – Nan and the chattering Great Aunts – would gather together to recount tales of familial happenings:

Nan: 'I remember when your Granddad first came 'ome…from the war that is….your moms…'bout five at the time, wouldn't go near 'im for about a week…didn't recognise 'im you see. Remember Maud?'

Maud: 'Ar… that's right. Mind you, Di (aunt) couldn't really care less… as long as she 'ad a packet of blackjacks she'd b'appy as Larry.'

All nod knowingly.

Jesse: 'You wouldn't 'ave guessed them pair were twins… would you Olive?'

Nan: Nods in agreement.

Jesse: 'Ar…chalk 'n cheese the pair of 'em. If I remember right, your Sandra (mom) only accepted your Edwin after 'e bought 'er that bicycle…y' know…the one 'e got from Sheila's son…what's 'is name?'

Minnie: 'Len'

Jesse: 'That's right!...Len, 'e used to 'ave that shop down Saltley Gate. Mind you…I never liked 'im…a bit of a shifty fella that one.'

All nod knowingly.

Nan: (looking puzzled) 'Don't be so daft…she was 18 when she 'ad that bicycle, Jesse.'

All (except Nan) nod knowingly.

Maude: 'Mind, she was shy. I think that's where young Lee gets it from. Aint that so young 'un?'

I blush. The others laugh!

Minnie: 'Ar… just like a tomato…just like 'is mom.'

My Nan and her sisters look at each other knowingly; they look at me lovingly and with approval. I know that they know and they know that I know – but nothing is said and nothing was said.

It was amid this vacuum of Nan's unequivocal love and recounts of familial history, that my own history – a silent history – would occasionally slip to the surface and although I knew of my adopted status, tacitly, their history became my history. When I did ask after the reasons behind my adoption, Nan would just smile warmly and say that I was a gift from god. Although Nan's answer satisfied my youthful curiosity, it also mystified the nature of my adoption – was I Jesus? My religious phase didn't last for long. But whilst I knew I wasn't the 'second coming', I also knew that there must be more to my adoption than what I was being told. Maybe I was too young to understand?

 As a teenager, the nagging constant of *not quite* being part of a whole was gently simmering in my consciousness, although, by this time, I had started to *use* my adoptive status when the need arose. This would usually take place after I had got into bother of one sort or the other and needed to sweet-talk Mom out of being mad at me. Well that's not quite right. I'd use it to sweet-talk Mom from telling Pat, (Mom's long-term boyfriend – or even our Step-Dad, but we never graced him with such a title) whose temperament was the reversal of Mom's quiet and kindly nature. However, these occasions had a dual purpose.

On one such evening, after setting fire to the 'dry' contents of the garden compost bin with a craftily, but recklessly disregarded cigarette, (in fact it was a joint – but the damage annihilated the evidence) I was sent to my bedroom to contemplate my misdemeanours and await my punishment from Pat, who, thank god, was out at the time. After waiting for what seemed an eternity and with only me, myself and I for company, I slowly made my way out of my dimmed bedroom and gingerly 'bottomed' myself midway down the stairs – just enough to gain a glimpse of Mom sitting at the dining room table thumbing through one of her much beloved gardening books. 'Mommm….where did I come from?'

Mom looked up at me and snapped: 'I don't know….but I know where you're going to!! Now get back upstairs, ya little sod.'

Not to be put off by Mom's initial rebuff, I harped on:

'Y' know Mom…where? Why did you adopt me? I could tell by the subtle softening of Mom's aggrieved expression that I had struck a chord. That single question had and was going to change to mood and direction of our banter.

'Look dear' Mom said quietly – knowing exactly the game I was playing. 'It's getting late. Go to bed and we'll talk in the morning.'

I knew that Mom understood what I was trying to do and I knew that if I carried on, Mom would make up an ulterior excuse for my pyrotechnical antics. But I *did* want to know more about why I was adopted. What Mom wasn't to know was that whilst rummaging through her wardrobe searching for Nan's old collection of family photographs, (long before the bin incident) I had discovered my original birth certificate. From this I managed to discover that my birth name was James Butcher, son of Beverley - a revelation – I now had a dual identity! More importantly though, was that I

had now uncovered evidence, though miniscule, of some reality of my Birthmother.

I knew a little more than what I was letting on – but this was beside the point.

'C'mon Mom…tell me now…pleasssse! Mommm! Why?'

Silence

Alternating her gaze from her book, to what remained of the deteriorating vista of our unpresuming semi-suburban neighbourhood; Mom seemed to be checking that it was clear to talk. Finally, with view and perhaps her mind clear, she turned her gaze towards me and stuttered:

'It's…well…it's complicated but when Bob and I were married (Bob is my adoptive father) we tried for a baby…but…there was a problem between us that meant that we could never have children of our own. So we chose you. Y' Nan and Granddad always used to say that you were a gift from god.' Mom's voice began to crack. Nan had died from Alzheimer's the previous year (hence the photographs in Mom wardrobe) and her loss was/is still heavily felt.

Composing herself, Mom began to tell me how she and Bob had gone to look for babies in the hospital.

'As soon as I saw you through the window I knew that you were the one. You were big and round and had a smile on your face.' Mom's voice began to flounder again. 'All the other babies were crying but you just lay there smiling….you were such a happy little soul.'

Silence

I didn't know what to say, or do – so I thought. I thought that I must have been special. They chose me and not one of the crying babies. Mom's emotions were telling me that it must have meant a lot to her – I must have been special. But why didn't my 'real' Mom want to keep me? With this thought I break the silence once again. 'Mom'.

'Yes dear'.

'Why was I in the hospital in the first place…I mean…what happened to my 'real'…Y' know…the lady who had me?' I was conscious of my Mom's feelings, and didn't in any way want to give the impression that I was ungrateful.

'Look, Lee…' Mom cooed protectively and in a drawn out manner. 'She was only young…I don't think she really knew what she was doing, but…she did want the very best for you…and, by giving you up for adoption…she did a very brave thing. It must have been really difficult for her.

Mom's answer, though reassuring, wasn't fulfilling. I wanted to know everything about this mysterious lady. Does she look like me? Does she think like me? How did she really feel about having to give me up? Did she want to give me up? Does she think about me now? Has she got any feelings towards me now? These and a thousand more questions flood my mind. But it's not just the questions that overcome me; it's the antagonistic feelings of anxiousness, excitement, sadness; it's the crippling feeling of wanting to know why? Why me? Why us? Why? Why? Why? It's the feeling you get when you're let down by the closest of friends; it's the feeling you get when your first love comes to an end. And, it's the feeling you get when you lose your Mom. How could I possibly explain this to Mom?

I never did get into trouble that night, but neither did I get any closer to the answers to my many questions. It was only with the passage of time and the retrogression of the subtleties of *truth* that the fractured narrative of my silent history and indeed my adoptive familial history, started to click, or let's say, scrape together.

Mom had separated with Bob shortly after I had been adopted. This I knew. The reason for their separation, according to Mom, always was simply because they had 'fallen out' and this is what I was told as a child. However, family history, as with life, or, the experience of life, can be messy. The fact was that shortly after adopting me, my Mom *was* to fall pregnant, but not by Bob, by his best friend – the father of my younger brother, Darren. The news of this created an emotional cataclysm, annihilating the relationship between both families. It was amid this atmosphere of deceit and treachery (and this is my estimation) that events surrounding my adoption became a family taboo – in essence my adoption became a taboo.

Mom, who had never told me these circumstances, instead confided in Darren – after all this was part of his own secret history too. Darren for his own reasons didn't tell me but confided in Tracey, his wife. It was only through the collusion of both Tracey and Debbie (my own wife) that the full truth was finally unearthed. And on a roll, possibly because she felt somewhat less burdened, Mom also decided to reveal once and for all the nature of my adoption. This act, however, was not to be undertaken by her, but by the passing of an old brown envelope to my brother who then in turn passed it on to Debbie – the final messenger. Still, in my hands I had the key to my past and perhaps my future. (Please see appendix for copy of my adoption document.)

It has been some eight years or so since I was handed that old brown envelope – its banal exterior giving no written clue to its hidden contents – yet this document, a single sheet of headed paper, contains all that I know and understand about the nature of my adoption and of my Birthmother and Biological father. I have read it a thousand times and on every occasion, impossible as it may seem, I glean something new from it; something that inexplicably hasn't already been burnt into my memory. Indeed it is the result of the latest new finding, the unearthing of a hitherto undiscovered sentence, which has bolstered my belief that the time has now come for me to search for my Birthmother.

The sentence influencing this belief:

'She really has found it very difficult to come to this decision on the baby's behalf and hoped that her parents might have helped her to keep him.'

I guess that to use the word 'undiscovered' when describing this sentence is somewhat inaccurate since, along with the rest of the text, it has been read by me over and over again. But what was it about Miss. J. I. Green's (Adoption Secretary) uneven type-set sentence that called out to me after such a lengthy period of hibernation? The reason, I think, lies in how it is to be interpreted.

Sandwiched between a physical description of my Birthmother and a short account her medical history, this oddly placed sentence could and was interpreted by me as the words of the young, but responsible Miss Green. (I can see her now – her slim frame sitting upright, hair in bun, typing away at her Silver Reed typewriter, stopping only momentarily to flick the return lever at the end of each line – austere, yet elegant!) But although they may be the words of Miss Green (or even the words of an invisible narrator, instructing Miss Green of her prose), they relay a different message to me now – that my adoption was unfortunately out of the control of my Birthmother, as it was with a lot of young girls of that era. It was probable that I was part of another family taboo, even before I was born and certainly afterwards.

They may have been another's words but surely they were influenced by my Birthmother's circumstances. I can only guess at what it must feel like for a mother to *have* to give away a newly born Baby – an entity carried inside, part of a mother's being – the feelings must be traumatic, irreconcilable, even guilt-ridden remorse and I also guess that my birthmother must have experienced these feelings too. It is only now, after 34 years of being betwixt, that my new-found appreciation that my 'giving away' **probably** did cause much and lasting trauma for my Birthmother, that I have felt a sense that I ought to search for her; to let her know things are alright; and that I don't blame her in anyway. I know only too well the complexities of **probably,** but without me confronting these complexities I will never know   the *certaintie*s of my own being.

The Diocesan Council for Family and Social Welfare

CHAIRMAN : THE RIGHT REVEREND THE LORD BISHOP OF EXETER

St. Olave's Church House, Mary Arches Street, Exeter EX4 3AZ   Exeter 59404

REGISTERED FOR ADOPTION

ADOPTION SECRETARY: MISS J. I. GREEN   CHAIRMAN OF ADOPTION COMMITTEE: THE REVD. P. H. LONGRIDGE, M.A.
Wednesday 10.30 a.m. to 12.30 p.m. or by appointment   The Rectory, Highweek, Newton Abbot
HON. DONATIONS SECRETARY: Mrs. E. G. MATHIAS, F.C.A., PENRITH, DOWN ROAD, TAVISTOCK

27th September, 1971.

Dear Mr. and Mrs. Pinfold,

I expect that this is going to come as a considerable shock, but we felt that we should write to you about baby James and give you the opportunity of considering whether he might be the right little boy for you to accept into your family. He is at present being fostered in Paignton and we are anxious that he shall be placed by the end of this week to avoid him having to change hands yet again. The foster mother goes away on Saturday so although we do not want you to feel rushed into making a decision, we will at the same time appreciate it if you would contact my colleague in Torbay as soon as possible (Telephone: Paignton 57733). If you do decide to see James, Mrs. Taylor would I am sure, be glad to bring him to her office at the Central Clinic, Midvale Road, Paignton, for you to meet.

James was born on the 30th June, 1971 at 10.30 p.m. in Torbay Hospital. He was then transferred to Shrublands with his mother and from ten days old he was looked after by his own mother in temporary accommodation in Brixham. After four weeks his mother felt unable to cope and asked that James should be fostered whilst she went back to her home in Somerset to try to sort things out. She has now written to ask that we proceed with adoption, as she realises that in the long run it would be in his best interests. He is a fine little boy, well built, and looks as if he is going to grow into a big lad. He has a round face, grey eyes, chestnut brown hair and a lovely skin. He seems to be an alert child, and is making very good progress. His birth weight was 7lbs. 2ozs. and his weight at the time of the medical exam (23.9.71) was 14lbs. 2ozs. The Guthrie test was done whilst in hospital and was normal, but the routine blood test has yet to be done. The mother's blood test taken on the 22nd June was negative. The medical report has been passed by our medical advisers. He is being fed on National Dried Full Cream Milk.

Beverley, the baby's mother, is aged eighteen, and although she comes from a very good family, she has led a somewhat 'way-out' kind of life, and has been in trouble with the police. She was sent to an approved school in Seaton for three years because she was beyond the control of her parents and she is at present on probation for having been involved in "borrowing" property belonging to her brother! She is now living at home again, where her father is a security officer at a power station; he has also been a swimming instructor and has taught mentally handicapped children. There are three brothers, one older and married with children, and two younger brothers still living at home and at school. There is also a twelve-year old sister who is at a school for blind, having lost her sight through the mother having german measles in pregnancy.

-2-

Beverley is about 5'8" tall, average build, with long brown hair, grey eyes, attractively pronounced teeth, and a cultured, deep speaking voice. She is a pleasant, friehdly girl, and although she is somewhat irresponsible, we have all been impressed with her warm and cheerful personality. She really has found it very difficult to come to this decision on the baby's behalf, and hoped that her parents might have helped her to keep him. The family doctor knows of no hereditary defects in this family's medical history, though he does state that Beverley herself went through an unsettled period in 1969 and indulged in various drugs during that time. This however, has not had any serious effects and has not been repeated in the last two years. Beverley is interested in art, dancing, crochet and knitting.

The baby's father is said to be an American aged thirty-one. He is 6' tall, average build, with fair hair and blue eyes. We have been unable to contact him and can tell you very little else, other than that he is divorced, has two children by his marriage, and was working for a firm of swimming pool constructors during the six months that Beverley was associating with him.

Needless to say I shall be anxious to know your decision, and would be grateful if you would advise me what you plan to do.

Best wishes to you both,

Yours sincerely,

Adoption Secretary.

The Sociologist

Richard Norrie

Laura sat at the table in a little cafeteria in the Lozells area of Birmingham. Days earlier the district had been rocked by riots which had been sparked by the rumour of the rape of a fourteen year old Jamaican girl by a gang of Asian youths at a beauty parlour. Two people had died in the ensuing troubles. Laura was a sociology student who had just come to the area to try and find out what were the underlying causes of the riot. She wanted to know what social factors had created a social environment that was similar to a shed full of dynamite, which would require just one spark to set it off. Laura was preparing a dissertation on the racial history of Birmingham. She was white, in her early twenties and came from a well-to-do middle class background. She was thoughtful on the inside but possessed a nervous temperament, so that she often did not express the full extent of what she was thinking. This was her first venture into the field. She was quite confident about how it would go. She was undertaking a trial-run; today she would just try and meet some people and try to establish some contacts.

Across the table from Laura sat a plump middle aged Jamaican woman. This was Laura's first interviewee. Laura was nervous and she fumbled with the switches on the Dictaphone that she had bought from the shops, only twenty-minutes before arriving. She had approached the woman, whose name was Doris and had offered her a cup of tea, on the condition that she could interview her. Doris was a plump lady with thick black curls that looked like they had been sculpted rather than styled. She looked as though she was a wise woman; the wrinkles on her face testified to this but they also pointed to an existence that had been shaped by anxiety. Once their tea arrived, Laura began to ask her questions. She had prepared some questions but was also quite prepared for the conversation to go to places that she had not anticipated. She believed in serendipity and thus had not prepared a rigid set of questions.

'Ok, thank you for agreeing to speak to me'. Being inexperienced, Laura thought that courtesy would stand her well.

'You're welcome,' said Doris. Doris seemed a little bemused by the situation. She had never been interviewed before.

'Now could you start by telling me a little information about yourself?' said Laura.

'What do you want to know?'

'Well perhaps you could start by telling me a little about your history.'

'Why do you want to know that?' said Doris. She was slightly uncomfortable with such questions coming from a white woman. She had lived through the Powell era and had come to consider questions regarding her history as being *really* questions about her legitimacy to live in the UK. Laura looked puzzled. She had not expected Doris's caginess.

'Emm...' she stuttered 'it's kind of important... I need to try and establish a connection with you... to try and get to the truth'. Laura revealed her idealism; she could not explain herself in any other words.

'You don't need no 'connection' with me' said Doris in a rather cross voice, but then she took pity on the young investigator who was squirming in her seat. 'Ok, I'll tell you. I was born in Jamaica in 1941. That makes me 64 years old. I came to England in 1962, just after the government closed the doors to Jamaicans coming to work here. They let me come because my husband was already here. He came here to build cars, at Longbridge. There's nothing left of the car industry now but it was great. People like my Derek made it great.'

'And why did Derek, your husband I mean, leave Jamaica?'

'There was no jobs back home, no opportunity, nothing.'

'And how was life for you? Here in England, I mean.'

'Hard. The racialism was hard. We Jamaicans were expected to do all the rotten jobs, jobs that white people didn't want. Then we were made into demons; they said we were lazy, dirty and stupid and they called us names. 'Nigger', 'Wog', they'd say 'go home to your own country''.

'That sounds terrible' said Laura.

'Yes. An' we Jamaicans were taught your English 'fair play'. All through school, they told us about the kindness of the mother country and white people go round with their noses up high. Pah!'

Laura was beginning to feel more confident. Doris was opening up to her. But then to her horror she noticed that the wheels inside the Dictaphone were not turning. She had pressed 'record' but she had somehow pressed down the 'pause' catch so that no recording was possible. Rather than adjusting the recorder, she carried on with the interview; she did not want to reveal her novice's mistake. She was also sketching out some notes on a spiral pad. 'Could you now tell me about the riots that happened last week?'

'It all started when those Asians forced the young girl... some twenty-five men they say'.

'And then what happened?'

'Well the fighting started and the Asians were all calling us names. It was scary; the police came down, but they came too late. They didn't want to get hurt. They don't mind so much if blacks are hitting each other.'

'Oh… I see,' said Laura. She was surprised at this. She was aware of the history of the policing of ethnic minorities, but surely things had changed now? Surely? 'Could you explain to me the general standard of race relations between Jamaicans and Asians?'
'Quite good, normally.'

*   *   *

Laura thanked Doris for her time. She paid for the teas and left the café in search of more people to interview. She saw a group of Asian young men standing on the street. She approached them, hoping to gain their perspective on things. There were five of them; two were leaning on a car whilst the other three were standing upright, facing them. They were well dressed and wore their hair cut sharply and neatly. As Laura approached them she felt a surge of fear. She thought of the girl. Had she really been raped? Maybe these men had done it? Could they rape me? As soon as she had these thoughts she felt guilty and admonished herself for falling into racial prejudice and stereotypes. But her initial thoughts remained at the back of her mind. She introduced herself to them. They were eager to talk. She started by recording their names and ages. The conversations were dominated by one man in particular, who appeared to be the leader of the group. His name was Ravi. He was tall and thin but possessed a wiry muscularity.
'There was no rape, don't believe them. What actually happened was that the business rivals of the guy who owns Beauty Queens spread these lies to discredit him. People are saying twenty men raped this girl, but there's not twenty Asians who would do that.'
'And what happened next?'
'Well the rumours spread and got bigger and then there's Jamaicans going crazy bricking Asian cars and firebombing our businesses. Then the fighting started between gangs.'
'And did you engage in any fighting?' Maybe this was the wrong sort of question, too direct, but Laura was a newcomer.
'No, not us personally, but we know some of the people who did. But most of the fighting was done by outsiders who had come to cause trouble. Some people are saying there were gangs from Nottingham and Bradford coming to cause trouble. Then one of our graveyards got desecrated. Muslim graves

were destroyed. A group called Black Nation did it, but some say it was the BNP trying to cause trouble, leaving leaflets behind to blame it on the blacks.'

*   *   *

After talking to Ravi and his friends, Laura was quite tired. She sat on a wall and looked through the notes she had taken. Her sentences were crude. When taking notes you have to hastily jot down the key words, ignoring grammatical rules. Laura realised that she would have to repair these broken sentences, relying on her own memory, if it were not for the Dictaphone. Laura thought about whether she would be able to represent what these people thought, or whether she would be just imposing her own beliefs and prejudices on them. She played back the interviews with Doris and Ravi. This was much better; here she had them, their real stories, in the palm of her hand, in the little black recorder. She resolved to use these stories intact without editing them at all. She wanted to give air to their testimonies, even though they contradicted each other. If she could not tell the truth about Lozells, perhaps they could. But then again, they were responding to her, an outsider whom they had no reason to trust. Perhaps the truthfulness of their stories was corrupted by a perceived need to please or reject her? Laura thought about what knowledge she would gather. Would she find out something about humans in general or just about the residents in particular? She thought that whilst she would develop some sense of what was going on, it would not be reality. Then it struck her that she didn't want reality. Her task was to condense reality because reality could not be fitted into a book or a blank page. She recalled her 2nd year lectures on theoretical ideas in sociology. The charismatic yet morose lecturer had spoken about Borges and his fable *'Of Exactitude in Science'*. Laura laughed as she remembered the people in the story who had created a map on a one to one scale. 'Absolutely useless' she said out loud. A woman with her children passing by, overheard Laura and gave her a dirty look. Science was about abstraction, that was unavoidable, but what was the right abstraction? To tell the truth about Lozells she would have to tell it on her own terms. These terms were moral choices, which only she could make. The question was, 'what truth do I want to show?'

*   *   *

Laura spent a couple of hours collecting further testimonies from other residents, whilst also exploring the area, to get a sense of the geography. It was important for her to be able to visualise the area in her mind. How could she write about a locale if she couldn't see it clearly in her mind? Next time she would bring a camera, to capture the unique character of the urban townscape. After some walking she saw an intriguing looking black man, wearing black jeans, a white shirt and a charcoal black corduroy jacket. He was in his early thirties and had a face that was contradictory. He

was baby-faced and yet there was a look in his eyes that spoke of experience; that said he had seen *and* understood more than most. Laura had the feeling that this man was an outsider like herself, but that he knew Lozells better than those who called it home. She approached him, how could she not?

'Excuse me, my names Laura Jones, I'm a sociologist and I'm researching the race riots. Could I please interview you?'

'What 'race riots'?' said the man. Laura was puzzled by his reply. Were her initial impressions of this man wrong? Where had he been the last few weeks?

'*The* race riots.'

'No. Let me correct you on this matter Miss Sociologist. There were no race riots here. A riot yes, but no race.'

'What do you mean?'

'I mean that the violence was carried out by rival gangs and extremist groups, not races. 'Race' is the adjective the newspapers give. Let me ask you this: is a football riot a race riot? When white people fight each other, is that a 'race riot'?' His voice was laced with contempt for the term.

'Oh, I see your point,' said Laura. She thought his analogy wasn't quite accurate but didn't want to press the point; she didn't like arguing with strangers and besides her task was to find out, not debate. She reached for her recorder. 'Do you mind?' Normally Efan would have dismissed her but as she had conceded his point, he was prepared to give her a chance. Laura's acquiescence had worked.

'Ok' he said 'but I ain't got much time.'

'Could you tell me your name and give me some details about your history?'

'My name is Efan, I'm Ghanaian. I grew up here, but I live in London now. I'm a writer.'

'What brought you back?'

'I'm here to promote unity. I'm handing out these leaflets.' He took out a leaflet, which had a picture of a black man and an Asian man standing together, both pointing at the camera with their fingers touching. Underneath was the caption 'Asians and Africans Unite! Prejudice & Poverty- a Common Enemy'. Laura looked at the leaflet; it puzzled her: 'If Asians and Africans have to unite, how can you say they are not disunited?' He smiled at her.

'Let me show you something.' He reached into his bag and took out a scrap book. Inside were newspaper clippings, related to the riot. 'Look at these headlines; look what they say.' One extract from *The Sun* read 'Clash of Cultures - Black and Asian rift explodes in deadly city riots'. Underneath

the article continued: 'Race is said to have played a part in the weekend riots in Birmingham. Not white against black, but Brown against Brown... Like the guns and the gangs, racism is abhorrent. There is no room for it in Britain, in any community... Asians and blacks in Birmingham's deprived Lozells district have lived for years in an atmosphere of distrust and hate.'

 'There's more' he said, passing her the folder. 'They're trying to stir up trouble, trying to create a situation and the reason they are doing it is to justify the presence of greater policing in black areas. The scheme of the racist state is to get the police into our areas so that they can harrass us more. The media is complicit in this.'

'Hang on' said Laura, 'we've got a Labour government now, things have changed from the Tory era?'

'We've got a Labour government but they are not in charge, it's the same old state, same old police and same old capitalists. We blacks are only wanted to do work whites don't want to do and they want to keep us in our place. When we do make advances they then undercut us by bringing in eastern Europeans, Poles. Listen I'm sorry if I was rude to you earlier but I'm suspicious of white bourgeois journalists, sociologists, anthropologists. They come down here and treat us like we are creatures in a zoo, animals to be gauped at and poked. They only come when there's a riot or a rape. The prospect of a riot caused by a rape must have sent them into raptures. At least you are a sociologist; have you ever noticed how they send sociologists to the white areas and anthropologists to black areas. They all have their own agendas. Either they are trying to measure us so we can be more efficiently controlled, or they are here just to prove to themselves that they are one of the *good whites*; not racist I mean.'

'But that's not me. I'm here because I care. I believe all people are equal and that everyone should be treated with respect, whatever their skin colour and by doing my research I'll be able to explain the things which oppress black people.' said Laura.

'Do you believe that? And even if your are authentic in your beliefs, what of the data you assemble. Who will be able to use it? Information circulates; once you've submitted it, it's beyond your control, your intentions become irrelevant.' Efan looked at his watch. 'I've got to dash, got a meeting.' Laura thanked him for his time. As he crossed the street, he turned and shouted to her 'Hey Miss Sociologist, ever get the impression we are just characters in some book, written by a white man?' Laura laughed. She was not sure what to make of Efan. She was both attracted to his anger but repelled by its power over her. She did not like the way it controlled her. The researcher can dominate the subject, but it can also be the other way round.

*   *   *

On the train back to her home town, Laura gazed out the window. It was still daylight and she was able to see the green pastures. She thought of the traditional England of old; the England of white men. Then she thought of how much it had changed over the centuries. She thought of what she had seen in Lozells. So many different people, each of whom could trace their ancestory across the globe. She thought of what had brought them here: job opportunities, love, the 'Motherland'. Then she thought of all the ways in which they had been marginalised and brutalised and yet had still changed the face of Britain so that it was unrecognisable, so that it was different. This was the truth she would show. Then she thought of herself. What had she learned from her experience? That difference was not to be taken lightly and that sociological investigation was not as easy as she had thought it would be; the world was not the bourgeois' playground and that working class people faced a 'real' world, a world where danger was more apparent and where violence was just a rumour away and not just hidden inside a television box or inside a book. Laura realised that her first attempt in the field had revealed to her more truth about herself than about Lozells. She had not discovered much about race relations; on the surface it seemed that everybody got on quite well. Doris was upset about the alleged rape but, about Asians in general, she seemed to have no complaints. Ravi was angry about the attack on the cemetary but held no tangible lasting anger toward the Jamaicans. Efan, the ideologue, was working to rectify the rifts but seemed to deny their existence. He seemed more angry at white people, or the state at least. Perhaps the essence of violence and hatred was always underneath the surface, festering away until something releases it and could not be accessed by a casual chat in a café. Or perhaps it was the work of outsiders after all. At last her train reached her stop. She was back on familiar soil. Home at last.

Annotated Bibliography

Richard Norrie

Ashcraft, K. & Mumby, D.K. (2004) *Reworking Gender: A Feminist Communicology of Organization.* London: SAGE.

> Postmodernism breaks the epistemological link between words and objects, suggesting that the meanings are conditional on other meanings; that meaning is 'deferred'. This raises questions for Laura; is she capable, as a sociologist, of capturing the real world by writing, or should she engage marginalised disciplines such as visual sociology to better convey the material world?

Banks, M. (1996) *Ethnicity: Anthropological Constructions.* London: Routledge.

> Banks says anthropology is either applied internally or externally; within the state it historically has asked 'are the migrants fitting in?' Banks shows that anthropology, like all sciences, cannot take its 'objectivity' for granted. He is saying that it has been an apparatus of the state and has served the interests of the powerful. This criticism is echoed in the arguments of Efan.

Caplan, P. (1993) 'Introduction 2: The Volume' from Bell, D. Caplan, P. & Karim, W.J. *Gendered Fields: Women, Men & Ethnography.* London: Routledge.

> Caplan sees a shift in feminist anthropology from trying to find commonality or 'sisterhood' with women, to finding and recognising difference. This shift coincided with the post-modern movement, which is primarily about difference according to Caplan. Caplan seems to think difference can be overcome and through this transcendence the truth can be grasped. My story suggests that commonality might be possible; Laura and Efan bond to some extent; but is that the aim of science, to be mates? Also the transcendence of difference may be impossible due to racist oppression; people, like Doris, get wise quick to the apparatuses of the bourgeois state and can be hostile. State racism leads to distrust, which will become apparent in researcher's interviews, like when Laura meets Doris.

Cesara, M. (1982) *Reflections of a Woman Anthropologist: No Hiding Place.* London: Academic Press.

> Cesara believes that the anthropological encounter between self and other is as much an encounter with your self or your past-selves. Falling back on a psychoanalytic framework, she argues that her encounters with the Lenda people allowed her to recover her repressed memories and identity, so that she recognised and challenged the cultural assumptions she took for granted. In Cesara's case, she loses her 'American' notions of a natural asymmetry of sexuality. In my story, Laura's investigation similarly proves to be a challenging experience. She finds out that she can be racist and that her task is not apolitical. The encounter with difference, paradoxically, lets you know just who you really are. Unlike Laura, Cesara is completely ignorant of the (potentially) political nature of her work. She is quite narcissistic, viewing anthropology as a chance to find herself and seems to believe that she can become one with the Lenda. My story hints at the power dynamic and privilege in the relation between interviewer and subject. Cesara believes difference can be transcended, but my story suggests that this is never the case, due to the possibility that the anthropological/sociological interview could be more than an encounter between self and other; it could be the encounter between disciplinary power and other (see entry on Foucault bellow).

Eshun, E. (2005) *Black Gold of the Sun: Looking for Home in England and Africa* London: Hamish Hamilton Ltd.

> The story of Eshun's life, as an exile from Ghana growing up in London. Eshun is an outsider from white society but also black Jamaican life, due to his middle class Ghanaian upbringing. Eshun searches for his roots but finds that his perceived identity differs from reality. This book shows the 'self' is constructed socially and that it is often a mystery to us; this problematises the anthropological task. How can one know the social environ through people, if they don't know themselves. The character of Efan is loosely based on Eshun.

Foner, J. (1979) *Jamaica Farewell: Jamaican Migrants in London.* London: Routledge.

> Helped with the history of Doris. If I were to write about 'the Other' I had to know something about them from historical sociology.

Postmodern anthropology would say that my knowledge is filtered by Foner then by me, so that my discourse loses contact with social

reality and instead becomes conditional on the other discourses active inside me. Efan's last line, where he asks if Laura thinks they live in a world invented by a white man, refers to the projection of myself onto 'the Other' which is one of the problems of modernist anthropology. This line also relates to the Foucaultian discourse of the decentred self, whereby 'the Self' is constructed by disciplinary power and not autonomously.

Foucault, M. (1991) *Discipline and Punish.* London: Penguin.
Foucault challenges the myth of the innocence of the researcher; are they in pursuit of 'knowledge' or are they the 'eyes' of the panoptical state, watching and recording everything in order to control it? Efan expresses similar ideas.

Golde, P. 'Introduction' in Golde, P. (Ed). (1986) *Women in the Field: Anthropological Experiences.* (2nd edition) Los Angles: University of California Press.
Golde raises issues that relate to the particular experiences of women anthropologists as women in patriarchal society. Women anthropologists are placed in a strange locale of a variable but universally patriarchal world, where they are potentially at risk. Anxiety is essential to the woman anthropologist's experience. In my story, Laura is scared of a gang of Asian men, but she is also torn because she does not want to succumb to racist myths. I wanted to show that an encounter with the 'Other' is an encounter with 'exotic' difference, with the real world, but also an encounter with one's self. Also the character of Efan is quite patronising to Laura. Is it because she is a woman? My story shows that no 'Other' has a monopoly of virtue.

Leonard, P. (1997) *Postmodern Welfare: Reconstructing an Emancipatory Project.* London: SAGE.
Postmodernism questions the adequacy of grand theories to represent the 'real' whilst dislodging Western 'scientific' authority. Leonard suggests that anthropologists often invent the 'real' and other 'the Other'. Postmodernism rejects notions of 'Truth', endorsing a dialogical empiricism which gives voice to a multitude

of stories, creating a collage of truth, with a small 't'.

Ratcliffe, P. (2004) *'Race', Ethnicity and Difference.* Maidenhead: Open University Press.

> Ratcliffe raises the point that difference is often invented or at least exaggerated for political reasons; something which Laura discovers.

Woods, T. (1999) *Beginning Postmodernism.* Manchester: Manchester University Press.

> According to Woods, post-modern anthropology questions representation, objectivity and the author reader relationship. It argues that modern anthropology masks the perspective of the subject by privileging the researcher's. Thus it is 'neo-colonial'. Instead post-modern anthropology embraces ambiguity, discord and heterogeneity. I tried to illustrate this with Laura's Dictaphone and her notes. The first is symbolic of the post-modern as it captures all of the subject's testimony, whilst the second is symbolic of the modern as it is Laura's order, imposed on her interviewees.

Zephaniah, B. 'The Angry Black Poet' in (1996) *Propa Propaganda.* Newcastle: Bloodaxe Books.

> This poem is about how journalists characterise Zephaniah as the stereotype of the angry black man. I was in danger of slipping into a similar stereotype with Efan. This highlights the dangers of representing difference in fiction. Postmodernism would say that this is also the case with non-fiction; that writers see things through their preconceptions. A Kantian defence would be that all knowledge is interpreted through a priori filters and that knowledge is only made possible by them. Perhaps one should say that some pre-conceptions are better than others or that they are good or bad depending on your politics. Laura comes to realise this.

Websites

Borges, J.L. *'On Exactitude in Science',* accessed 28/04/2006.
http://www.econ.brown.edu/~iph/pdf/Borges.pdf.

> In this fable, Borges makes the point that capturing reality completely through science is really a nonsensical proposition. Laura learns this lesson whilst out in the field. She embraces the post-modern critique that social-science cannot tell the truth and

only can work on abstractions, which are determined by the researchers political and moral outlook.

'The So-Called Lozells Riots' accessed 21/04/2006.

This article is the source for my knowledge of the Lozells Riots. It also is of importance as it raises questions about the political agenda of mainstream media, which led me into a Foucaultian discourse. Laura is challenged by Efan, who wants to know her agenda. It also conveys how difficult it is to establish what happened in any event; it shows how there are conflicting testimonies and that what is reported is an abstraction which reflects the ideology of the abstractor.

Ujalli

Natalia Shpakovata

I came to Rajasthan to collect stories. How ridiculous, to think about it, that we Bengalis always think ourselves to be ever so different from other Indians, better somehow. At the University of Kolkata we call ourselves anthropologists and go and study 'the natives'. We are so proud of our independence but really, we study the poor and the illiterate of our own land like the British once studied us! I did my research on the Internet and was happy when sites claimed that Rajasthan is 'impressive and fascinating, it is packed with history, arts and culture'. So, I came to observe a rural community and then tell stories of illiteracy and ignorance, set against the backdrop of colourful skirts, merry festivals and cheerful traditions, to my colleagues and perhaps compile a delightful little book called something like 'Simple People of Rajasthan' or 'Land of Colours'. Neat!

I arrived to one of the thousands of look-alike villages in the middle of Thar Desert late at night, tired and irritated with the dry heat so unlike the humidity of Bengal. I was met by one of the elders, Sakhram Thakur, who accommodated me in his own house, sharing a room with his sons. I was surprised – the house had a tiled roof and solid wooden floors, while my expectation was a picture from a cheap Bollywood movie – mud huts, sleeping on the floor and total absence of basic comforts. I fell into heavy sleep and dreamt of going back home to the comforts of my ma's milky sweets and my wife's intoxicating embraces. I did not know that I will wake up to find a story I do not know how to tell, which made me travel back to Kolkata determined to give up ethnography.

Rajasthani village is a colourful place. Absence of greenery and water is amply compensated for with intricate colourful designs on walls, fences, clothes, turbans… The house I was staying in is actually one of very few '*havelis*', others are plain mud huts. The heat here is made even more unbearable by the smells – drying cow dung cakes slapped onto the walls of the huts, spices being fried in *ghee*, sick goats, neglected kids, roasting *besan*, sweaty men and coconut oil in the hair of every single inhabitant, all contribute to the sweetly, sickening scent. There is a sort of raw beauty here, something so basic and natural that makes poverty and stench somehow romantic. I felt transported to an age long gone and for some hours meditated on the beauty of a simpler life.

But something is wrong there. I did not recognize it at first, a dark presence hanging over the desert, something strange and unnatural in this simplicity. The women… At first it was strange to see so few in the lanes of the village. Even those who ventured out covered their faces with *dupattas* and almost ran to their destinations. So different from my native Bengali villages! I steadied myself, as a good ethnographer, not to make any hasty conclusions. But I could not help noticing that even though Bollywood has created a right image of the colourful embellished clothing of these women, their exquisite 'ethnic' jewellery, their face *mehendis*, something is wrong. The actresses in the ever popular Rajasthani settings carry their costumes so easily, so gracefully, but so many of these village women remind me of the cows fancily decorated with colourful trinkets before slaughter during Ramadan. Young wives' bodies do not yet fill their blouses and they look like they are playing with their mothers' clothes, until you see their faces - teenage girls marked with sins of old men…

But I am not a feminist. I did not come to Rajasthan to fight for the rights of its women. I have never really come in contact with things like *sati* or rape punishments and I ignored my own unease, like so many of us do, watching beautiful black babies starve to death on TV while we enjoy our evening *chai* and *rosogollas*. I spent most of my first day in the village trying to pick up conversations with people (fruitlessly), trying to observe their domestic lives (fruitlessly) and making notes in my research diary (not very usefully, either). I was irritated and restless. And then I saw her.

She was walking out of an old hut that I assumed, on my inspection of the village, to be uninhabited and I remember wondering what a little girl was doing there, before I almost choked on my *chai* as I noticed her white *ghagra choli*. No woman, especially in this part of India, would ever wear all white, scared of attracting bad fate – she was a widow. She walked with her head uncovered and people stared. She had a face of a child – so clean, so pure, still rounded with baby chubbiness and her cheeks had a hint of pinkish blush, rare to the dark brown skins of the desert. But there were wrinkles around her eyes and under them – pools of darkness. Her fair face was framed with extremely black hair, streaks of grey on her temples. It is hard to imagine a little girl with grey hair. But I saw one and I would not wish the sight to my worst enemy. She held a small child and I hoped with my whole heart it was not hers.

She passed me without a second look as I kept staring. When I finally managed to come to my senses, a few inquiries produced a background – her name was Ujalli, the widow of Mangilal Seth, the child she held was her daughter Lachchi and she lived with her father Chandralal, educated in England, who is the village madman and is rumoured to have not spoken a word for the last 5 years. All I could find out about the girl's mother was that she was a foreign lady whose life ended 'as she deserved'. My irritation was quickly gone as I imagined that I have found a perfect family to study – the mystery of a foreign mother, the tradition of child marriage, effects of early motherhood, creation of the madman reputation in rural society… I did not waste time in approaching my setting and within half an hour was knocking on Chandralal's door.

-          Jay Ramji!

I tried to establish trust by greeting him in local Rajasthani dialect. No answer. I came in. He was sitting on the floor, slowly taking little pieces of *chapatti* from a newspaper cone and dipping them into thin *daal* before placing them into his mouth with an empty expression. Chandralal was a postcard-type old man. His skin was still evenly coloured chocolate, shiny and perfectly wrinkled all over his face and hands. He boasted a bushy white moustache and wore a huge multicoloured turban. From what I gathered in the village he could not be more than 40 but looked 80. He lifted his head to look at me and I saw fear in his eyes, like a hurt animal that no longer trusts anyone.

> - Jay Ramji! My name is Bahadur Roy; I have come from Kolkata University to conduct an ethnographic study in your village. I wondered whether you would mind if I interviewed you.

He kept dipping pieces of *chapatti* in *daal*. I sat down on the floor near the door and told him more about myself, hoping to establish some connection - about my education, my family, why I was fascinated with Rajasthan. I told him that I wondered about his daughter's life. He remained silent and I finally left late at night. The same happened the next day. I sat with Chandralal the whole day, hoping that he would get used to my presence and talk. Ujalli came in several times, bringing water and food, sweeping floors, pacifying her baby. She never spoke except for soft sounds she made to her daughter. I wondered whether she loved Lachchi, if she understood her motherhood. Did she know any love at all or was her heart hard as stone by now? How did her father let this happen? I tried to be patient and kept asking questions, by the end of the day no longer hoping for an answer. It drove me mad that he would not talk, would not explain. I felt important, 'studying' important social problems. That day was probably the last one in

my life when everything in the world was divided only into black and white.

By the end of my second day of observing Chandralal eat his *chapatti*, drink his *chai* and smoke his *hookah* and staring at Ujalli move like an efficient machine around the house, I could not bare it any longer and I shouted at him, in English:

- Why will you not talk?! Are you scared? How can you call yourself a man? To hell with you!

I stormed out, forgetting all the ethics and objectivity of a good ethnographer, determined to at least report him to police for dowry giving and child marrying and at most to murder him.

*   *   *

On my third morning in the village, I watched my host's servant try very hard not to pass on the latest village gossip as he served me *chai, chapatti* and *halva*. Within 10 minutes he could not take it any longer and smiling coyly sat at my feet.
- Sahib, have you heard what happened?
- No, Bhoja, but you have become my morning newspaper so you might as well tell me.

I expected the usual – marriages, dowries, rows, births, his wife's new silver bangles… As he steadied himself for his big news, I was planning my day and hoped to apologize to my silent subject for my outburst.

- The *madwallah* jumped in the well with his daughter and her child at night. Told you he was mad! Anyway, Thakur thinks he will take his land. And I did get my wife those bangles I told you about, the ones with the little bells. Oh and he left a letter that no one can read, probably in English or some mad language, you should go and have a look, you are educated. Drowned, all of them; he tied a stone to his neck and held them both tight, they say.

*   *   *

'Dear *Babu*,

Thank you for your visits. You were the first person to visit us in months. You are so eager… I used to be like you, long ago. What could I tell you,

what stories for you to write down? Were you looking for clichés of poverty, ignorance and illiteracy? My dear sir, I graduated from Oxford and was married to an English girl. But look what I did… I will tell you a little story before I go. A story of how one man killed three women. My wife, my daughter, my granddaughter. Read this and go back home, study somewhere easier. This place is not a semi-serious setting for work of doubtful quality and purpose. You cannot help. And do you really want to?

I met my wife, Mary, in England and to be honest, hoped for a bit of fun with a white girl before going back home. But by chance or destiny, my first bit of fun turned into something wonderful – we fell in love after just a couple of weeks. She was so innocent, so amazingly happy about life, she glowed with such light that I could not but be drawn to her. I knew I was in huge trouble. I could not take her back home. I decided to stay, look for a job. But my father died and I had to go back to take care of the family or maybe I wanted to. By then we were married and Mary just found out she was pregnant. I was already a coward then; I packed secretly and left in the middle of the night... and came back from the airport. I could not leave her and my baby. My little heroine… she packed her few *sarees* and went with me.

Even now, ready to meet her in the next incarnation, I can't write in detail about her life here. I will tell you this – they could not stop us marrying but they could stop us being happy. She never told me exactly what was happening to her, what they said, what she heard, how she felt when she found out she was expecting a girl. I saw her melt and change but I did not face it. They called her a whore to her face, every day. They said her child was a product of sin. They told her she could not even bear a son, she proved she was trash. They claimed I was looking for a proper wife… if she held on before, after birth she could not. When Ujalli was just a few days old, she set herself on fire in the kitchen.

I cremated her remains, walking the circles around the fire, again. The first time she was behind me, the edge of her red *saree* tied to my shawl, her eyes down, so proper a bride. She was only 25 when the waters of the holy Ganges carried her ashes. I looked on but could no longer feel the pain. Then suddenly I saw a tiny piece of sky-blue fabric floating among the ashes. It might have already been there… but to me it was a piece of her blue *saree,* the first one she ever wore. Over the years, back in England, it grew old and was covered in stains from all the delicacies she cooked, but

she never threw it out. I started walking towards the blue, which seemed to grow larger and larger with every step, just to put my face in her lap once more, smell sandalwood smoke from the morning *puja*, cumin seeds frying in *ghee*, jasmine soap where she wiped her hands after washing… I wanted to keep following that little piece of fabric, hoping it would lead me to her, but I was young and still scared of death, so I brought up Ujalli until she was 10. As they talked about her mother, they talked about this child. They did not allow their children to play with her. They cursed her beauty. They punished her for the sin of her mother's difference. I wished I left her in England… our family lost all its money and status by then, we could barely eat and when my brother suggested we marry her off, I did not object. I did not even care much. This is the way things were always done, I thought, it's for the best. Old widowers were our choices, tempted by her fair beauty, for what house will marry their young son to a daughter from such a family?

She was married during the festival of Akhai Teej, an astrologically auspicious date, one of the thousands of illegal weddings ignored by the police that day. I almost wished there was a raid, but then I thought we are not the worst off – she is already 10, some are marrying their babies off. I tried not to wonder how long do middle aged husbands wait before… but, my friend, I was, and remain, a coward and learned not to think too much. We all have. When one of those activist women visited our village, our own women laughed at her and men told her to go away. You know, Ujalli was happy. She had many *laddus* and fell asleep during the holy chants and my own relatives congratulated me on becoming free of the curse bestowed by my wife as they ate the goat meat I sold Mary's only gold bangles for.

We sent her to Mangilal's house the next day. My brother and I could not afford to keep her any longer. So here, sir, I am an old pimp. I gained a few rupees by giving my child to an old man to molest. They say education is the way forward. I went to Oxford! We try to excuse our traditions, saying that they came from the time when Moguls raped unmarried girls so they had to be married early to be protected… true or not, fathers of girls are eunuchs, then. I got dead drunk that night, not to think what he was doing to her. Perhaps in the other world Mary will turn away from me, knowing what I have done.

Mangilal lost interest in Ujalli after she had Lachchi, when she was 13. She irritated him he said and brought her back to me. I could not keep her. So he sold her to one of the Thakurs as a concubine and with the money he got, bought himself a new 12 year old from parents who could not even afford to get her married. Ujalli got a room in Thakur's *haveli* and kept her child with her.
I think she was much happier there then with her husband. She became fatter and brought savouries for me when she could. But the child was ill and cried at night and Thakur threw her out of the *haveli*. She came to me, begging to take her in, swearing to earn money to feed us all in any way possible. It was the last time she ever cried. When me and my brother turned her away, she stopped weeping and went back to her husband. They said he kept her to sell, but she never confirmed this and I do not want to ask.

The bastard died soon after Ujalli came back, he was at least 65. His family sighed about the good old times of *sati* but did not dare force her. I think she would be happy to have an excuse to die without sin, if she did not have Lachchi. Funny, does she need to live to see her own daughter become a mother in few years? Not for her to prevent that! Perhaps she did not do it, even if she wanted to, just because an established Rajput tradition dictates that a wife's *sati* is in honour of the fallen hero husband and she hated him, hated him bitterly, so much that I think sometimes she hates Lachchi too, as his seed.

She was in love once, you know. When she lived in the *haveli,* the rumour went around about her and Lakhan, a homeless 16 year old who helped with the goats. I do not know what happened, but one night he disappeared. Even though she only wore white after her husband died, she broke her bangles then and the last bit of light that was left in her just drained away. It is also then, not even when she was pregnant or sold, that her hair started turning white…

You are a good man, dear Bengali *Babu*! Go home. Teach middle class kids about Marx and Weber, eat good food, talk cleverly about poverty but stop trying to live it. Perhaps one day there will be happiness for girls like my Ujalli and I hope that day you remember us and raise a glass of wine in one of your old colonial clubs to our health in the new incarnations. Go home and make love to your wife every night, knowing that life sometimes is too short. Bring your sons up as good men and your daughters - able to fight. Ujalli is not a fighter, same as her mother, but she remains the light of my life, just too good and too hurt to shine in this dark world. But she will, somewhere, some day.

Goodbye.'

*   *   *

I left for Rajasthan eager to tell stories afterwards but came back wanting to be silent. I could not bear the thought of this beautiful child that knew too much being discussed as just one of the millions of helpless girls this land has swallowed, grinded to dust over the years. The cycle goes on… some little girl is being married to an old man right now and another teenager is having her hair cut off in widowhood. I love India fiercely. I was sarcastic about patriotism as a teenager and hated India for its backwardness, for holding us back. I am still no patriot, but at some stage I fell in love with this country, perhaps when I saw my wife fall in love with it, seeing everything through her eyes, finding beauty in dirt. India intoxicates. Its extremes of wealth and poverty, beauty and repulsiveness, goodness and evil, lure you into the world you can never leave, make you greedy for its pleasures. I have fallen in love on many occasions – with endless rivers, with sensual temples, with its food, its gold, often its people. I have also hated India, but I do not feel hatred now, towards this hidden world far behind the cities of golden lifestyles. I feel deceived and somehow resigned. Am I responsible? Would he not have done it if I never came? Or is it better this way?

Last night I walked the miles to town and the journey back to Kolkata seemed to take years. It was late by the time I arrived home. My brothers were watching football in the living room and I could hear the voices of my *baudis* from one of the bedrooms. I opened the door but she was not there and I panicked. What if something happened to her? I brought her here; I should never leave her alone…

Our room was tidy as usual when I am not there, her pretty little boxes and figurines displayed in all their glory, fresh flowers on the table, incense smoking slowly. It was almost a shock to be back to the world where women wear made to order gold ornaments, designer *salwars* and Dior perfume, after the one where little girls die. I sat down and wrote my story, right now, such quick ethnography! What do I know about her? What can I know? Do I have the right to even talk about her? Perhaps one night I will leave this on the bed for my wife to read. Not now. Later. But I need her to know, I need to share the weight of this. Or maybe one day I will follow the illusion of fame and publish just another story of another girl... Outside, it is still dark and the air is heavy with the mysteries of India.

*   *   *

I lie down beside her, smell her milky white skin, cup her rounding belly and try to feel the little heartbeat inside, my golden child... I swear to God to protect her, both of them, forever. What if I can't? I want to take them away. This world does not accept difference and I do not know what to do. I cry into waves of blond hair for hours and when she wakes up she holds me and does not ask.

GLOSSARY

Babu – respectable form of address, sir.

Baudi – elder sister, sister in law (Bengali).

Besan – lentil flour.

Chai – traditional tea prepared with milk, sugar and spices.

Choli – short embroidered blouse worn with Ghagra (see below).

Dupatta – large scarf worn with ghagra choli to cover the front of the body and the head (and often face).

Ghagra - long wide skirt worn by Rajasthani women.

Ghee – clarified butter.

Haveli – palace, grand house.

Hookah - water pipe.

Laddu – a round sweet prepared for special occasions, usually made of chickpea flour or semolina with ghee and sugar.

Mehendi – henna.

Puja – worship, prayer, religious celebration.

Rosogolla – traditional Bengali sweet balls made with cottage cheese and soaked in rose-scented syrup.

Sati – controversial custom of supposedly voluntary widow self-immolation on the funeral pyres of husbands.

Thakur - member of the highest caste, landowner, Rajput.

Ujalli – light (Hindi/Rajasthani).

Stuart's Story

Alison Fisher

What was the matter with me?

Why couldn't I recognize words?

Was I stupid?

How come everyone else appeared to think that reading was easy?

These were the kinds of questions that I asked myself daily. I was twelve years old and I'd grown up surrounded by books. I loved to hear stories and I loved art, music and drama. I dreamed of working in a theatre, not necessarily acting, although that appealed to me too, but I would love to be involved with the scenery and the special effects. However, a dream was all it was. I was never going to pass enough exams to even allow me to work in Burger King, never mind the theatre! My mother was a lecturer and my father was a solicitor, the house was like a library. For as long as I can remember my mother had shared stories with me, but when it came to enjoying these stories on my own, well, there was no chance. They were out of bounds. I was surrounded by books and yet access was strictly prohibited. My teachers thought I was stupid, I could tell and I could imagine what they would say about me at the open evening.

'Stuart needs to try harder. Capable of better work. Doesn't seem to have progressed at all this year, etc, etc.' I'd heard it all before. However, now my parents were buying what the school was saying and they seemed to think I was messing around too. Nobody seemed to understand what I was trying to tell them. Maybe they were right. Maybe I was stupid.

Pam's Story

What is the matter with him?

Why can't he remember simple words?

Was he being bullied at school?

Was he just not bothered?

These were the kinds of questions I asked myself daily. My twelve-year-old son was bright, with a vivid imagination, brilliant at art, but apparently totally incapable of remembering even the simplest of words. To say that he frustrated me was an understatement. I loved him dearly and always encouraged him to do well, but this first year at secondary school was proving to be the most torturous time. According to the school, his reading age was that of a nine year old. He could be told what a word was on one page, then turn the page and stumble on the same word! Why? I knew he was capable of better. It was as if he just wasn't trying, yet his art report was brilliant. No spelling or reading involved in art though, was there?! What was to become of Stuart? Maybe we could try extra lessons again; he might have been a bit young to benefit from them last time. I'd mention it to his tutor at the open evening.

David's Story

What was the matter with him?
How was he going to earn a living, if he couldn't even read?
Was he involved with some girl?
These were the kinds of questions I asked myself from time to time. Stuart was my twelve year old son and the cause of many a heated argument between my wife and I. He wasn't a bad child, but his academic achievements to date were poor to say the least. I expected more. He had attended an excellent primary school, but had failed to make the grade. Now he had gone to secondary, he was just another fish in the ocean. Totally lost, 'Mr. Average,' 'nice but dim', that was Stuart. He'd had private tutors, his mother was a lecturer, but he still couldn't grasp anything but the simplest reading. He needed to knuckle down and stop making excuses. He was alright if it involved drawing or constructing, but anything more challenging, he didn't want to know! I couldn't wait to hear what his teachers had to say this time.

Mr. Miles' Story

I hope that Stuart's parents come to see me this evening. Not everyone bothers with the art teacher; they tend to concentrate on the 'important subjects', namely english, maths, IT and sciences. Stuart was in his first year at Heartlands School and I had been teaching him art for three months now. He was a bright boy, with a real talent for art and a vivid imagination. But it was the content of his work that I wanted to show his parents. I was worried that there was a problem that Stuart wasn't telling anyone about. I'd talked to my colleagues and discovered that he was struggling in his academic subjects, but he was more than willing to participate in any practical work. They all agreed that he seemed to be capable of more. I wondered if he might be dyslexic. I wanted to meet his parents and see if they would be receptive to this idea. The Headmaster had agreed and I felt that if I could talk to them and show them his artwork, they might give my suggestion some thought at least. I was speaking from experience, because

I was dyslexic myself. I wanted to show Stuart and his parents that you didn't have to be written off, that there was hope, but first of all the problem needed to be diagnosed.

Parents Evening. Heartlands School 6.30pm.
 'Didn't think you were going to make it, was the traffic bad again?' Pam slipped her arm through David's as she asked him the question.
 'No, traffic was OK, just tying up last minute details for tomorrow's court case. How was your day?'
 'Fine, fine. I've been thinking about tonight mostly. I thought we might ask the tutors about extra tuition for Stuart again, what do you think?'
 'Pam, if I thought it would actually do any good, I'd hire one full time, but nothing seems to make a difference. I don't understand how two reasonably intelligent people like us, managed to produce such an idiot.'
 'He's not an idiot!! David how can you say that about Stuart? He's not an idiot.'
 'Well he's not a bloody genius either is he?'
David's forehead furrowed with exasperation as he strode towards the school entrance. Pam's arm had returned to her side, as she walked a few steps behind him. David turned as he reached the door and let out a deep sigh.
 'I'm sorry, Pam. He just annoys me. I don't understand his behavior, his attitude. I don't want to argue again.'
 'Let's hear what his new teachers say, we might be pleasantly surprised.'
They both smiled and walked into the school.
As usual the appointments were running a little late.
 'Maybe we could go and see the art teacher now, while we're waiting. We shouldn't be with him too long.' Pam suggested.
 'Yes. At least I suppose we'll be starting off on a positive note. I don't think he's ever had a bad art report. Just english and history and geography…..'
 'David.'
 'Sorry. Really, I'm sorry'
 'He won't improve if you're on his back all the time. I've told you before, you need to praise him, not just get on at him.'
 'Sorry.'
Then under his breath, David muttered,
 'Just a pity there's nothing worth praising him for.'
The walls in the art block were covered with students' work. Pam and David were looking at one large painting that had Stuart's name underneath it, when they were approached by Mr. Miles.

'Good evening' he introduced himself and showed them to his classroom, where he started to empty the contents of Stuart's folder as he talked.

'I'm really glad you came to see me tonight Mr. and Mrs. Tomney, there's a particular piece of work that I want you to see.'

'Oh God, he's probably drawn something pornographic. I won't even be able to praise him for his art now!' David whispered to Pam.

'Here it is' Mr. Miles announced as he pulled the picture from Stuart's folder. It was a charcoal picture of a face, well mainly a mouth. A large, open, black mouth. It looked like a picture of someone screaming, except that the rest of the facial details were faint, it was mainly a mouth. It was a picture of a scream. What made it interesting was that the face/scream was drawn over old school reports that looked like they had been burnt, as they were singed at the edges. They had been stuck all over the paper and this face/scream had been drawn on the top.

Pam and David reached out and took the picture from Mr. Miles.

'Those are Stuart's old reports,' announced Pam

'How did he get them? I thought you kept them in your trunk?'

'I do. Well, I mean I did. Obviously I don't have them any more, because they're here.'

'I hope I haven't got Stuart in any trouble' interrupted Mr. Miles, 'I assumed he'd had permission to use them. But that's not really the issue here. The reports are all less than complimentary about Stuart's work; I think that's the point. Stuart is showing his frustration with his learning difficulties through his art work.'

'Learning difficulties. What learning difficulties? This is news to us. We know he's not exactly cut out to be a nuclear scientist, but what's all this learning difficulty nonsense?' David seethed.

'Let me explain' Mr. Miles said in a calm voice. 'Please, if you could just listen to what I have to say. I won't take up much time.'

'I think you'd better explain….'

'That'll be fine, please go ahead,' Pam interrupted.

'I recognize some of the problems that Stuart is having with his academic work because I suffered from them myself when I was at school. I believe that Stuart may be dyslexic.'

'Dyslexic.' Pam and David said together.

'Yes, I think it's possible. From talking to my colleagues, Stuart seems to display some classic symptoms. His reading and spelling is below average, he has problems with planning an essay, yet he's very alert and a bright talented pupil in subjects such as art.'

David and Pam stared at Mr. Miles. Their eyes were fixed on the painting.

'I don't believe Stuart is stupid or lazy, he genuinely can't recognize the letters on the paper. It doesn't have to be like that for ever.

There are different techniques that he can use. The next step is to get an official diagnosis. We can arrange for a test to be done through the LEA.' Pam and David were looking at Mr. Miles now.

'If he is dyslexic, why has it taken so long for it to be picked up? He's gone all through primary school, struggling, when he could have had help, is that what you're saying?' Pam asked with tears in her eyes.
 'Mrs. Tomney, I can recognize and sympathize with Stuart, because I am dyslexic. I'm not in a position to officially diagnose it, but as a fellow sufferer, I feel qualified to pick up on the signs. Trust me, the sooner Stuart gets help, the happier he will become.'
 'You say you've discussed this with your colleagues, when were you all thinking about discussing it with us? We are after all his parents.'
 'Mr. Tomney, this picture was produced just last week especially for parents evening. I asked the pupils to express how they felt about school in a picture. This is what Stuart produced. I talked to his tutor and the Headmaster and we agreed that I could approach the subject with you tonight. The school wants to help, really.'
 'I'm sorry. It's just a bit of a shock that's all.' David rubbed his temples.
 'It's a bit of a relief actually. I had never thought about the possibility of dyslexia before' Pam said, turning to the picture. 'Could we take this home? It might help when we talk to Stuart.'
 'Yes, yes, of course.'
 'That's a good idea.'
 'Have you seen Stuart's tutor yet?'
 'Not yet, no.'
 'Shall I make an appointment for you both another time? Maybe when you have had a chance to talk to Stuart about how he feels?'
 'Could you do that? That would be great. Thank you.'
 'Come with me' Mr. Miles smiled and led the way to the Headmaster's office. After a brief chat, an appointment was made to discuss Stuart's progress and make an appointment with the LEA for an assessment. Pam and David left the school with a pamphlet about dyslexia and Stuart's painting.
 'He's not getting bullied then, he's actually got a problem.'
 'He's not lazy, or involved with a girl either.'
 'I think we've got some long overdue listening to do!'

The Tomneys' house. 7.30pm

Stuart was watching a holiday programme with his Nan when Pam and David returned home.

'Hello dear, hello David, everything alright?' asked Nan.

'Hello Mum. Yes everything's fine. Thanks for coming round' Pam replied as she gave her Mum a hug and a peck on the cheek.

'Alright mate' she continued as she turned to Stuart and hugged him too.

'I'm fine. How was school?' Stuart asked tentatively.

'School was good. Very good.' said David, walking towards Stuart with his picture held in front of his chest.

'I'll be going' said Nan 'I'll be home in time for Eastenders. I'll see you at the weekend.'

'Bye Nan' Stuart said as he kissed her cheek.

'Bye Mum'

'Bye Betty'

'Bye Dears'

Stuart's heart was pounding. Something had obviously gone on at school, but he was unsure what. Was Dad serious when he said his report had been good? Or was he really in trouble for using his old school reports to draw on? Stuart had thought that his parents might not visit the art block, or even if they had, that they wouldn't pay too much attention to the contents of his folder. He was puzzled.

'Oh Stuart' his Mum sighed as she hugged him. 'Come and sit down, let's turn the telly off and talk.'

Stuart was convinced that this was going to be another 'you're capable of more' talks. He sat on the sofa with his Mum, his Dad settled on the chair next to him. The smell of Nan's perfume still lingered in the air and Stuart wished she was still here. That may have delayed this talk.

'Stuart', David reached out his hand and rested it on his son's knee, as he talked. 'We're sorry.'

This wasn't what Stuart had been expecting.

'Sorry?'

'Yes, I think we owe you an apology for getting on at you for so long, don't we Mum?'

'Certainly do.' Pam's eyes were filling with tears. 'Oh Stuart.'

'What's the matter?'

Stuart was beginning to panic slightly now. His parents were acting strangely. He wasn't sure if he liked this talk better than the usual kind of school open evening talks, or not.

'Mum, why are you crying?'

'We talked to Mr. Miles and the Headmaster and your tutor. They think that the reason you're struggling so much with your work is because you may be dyslexic. After they talked to us about it, we saw more and more signs of it in your behaviour, even as a small child. Apparently, one of the classic signs of dyslexia in young children is jumbling up phrases. Do you remember the way you used to say things Stuart? Do you remember? It was always 'papost' instead of postman, and 'cobblers club' instead of toddlers club!' 'Yeah, and 'pottom' instead of bottom. I remember!'

'Yes, yes, 'pottom', of course, how could I forget that one! Oh, Stuart, we're so sorry for giving you a hard time. We just didn't know. But now we can help you properly. You'll be OK mate.' It was David's turn to cry now.

Stuart stared at his parents in bewilderment. He'd heard of dyslexia, but didn't really know what it was. A girl at school had it and used blue tinted glasses to read with.

'So what does that mean then?' asked Stuart.

'It means that you have to do some tests that the school will organize for you. They will tell us what kind of dyslexia you have and then you will be taught different techniques to help with your reading and writing.'

'It takes time though, mate. You won't just go to school tomorrow and be able to read because you know you're dyslexic. Apparently there are a lot of different techniques that can help; you just have to find the ones most suited to you.' David smiled at his son as he spoke.

'You'll be able to read all these books for yourself, in time, Stuart.' Pam looked lovingly at her son.

'Really?'

'Yes, really.'

'Do you think I'd be able to pass enough exams to work in the theatre?' David and Pam glanced briefly at each other and then turned to Stuart.

'I'm sure you can. You're not stupid darling, you just need help and now Dad and I are going to make sure that you get it! If you want to work in the theatre, then go for it!'

'Wow!' David exclaimed. 'I'm not stupid then, I'm dyslexic!'

All three laughed, as they hugged each other, tears streaming down their cheeks.

Just like you

Claire Pattison

A girl who seems to be of a similar age to me walks past. She seems well dressed and is laden with bags containing her purchases from the high street stores. It's midday, on no particular Tuesday and I'm sitting on a bench in the middle of town just watching the world go by while I eat my lunch. I'm here minding my own business, but she's noticed me. There is an awkward moment when it dawns on her that I have noticed her looking. She turns away; it's easier to pretend she doesn't see me. I know she didn't intend to come my way, it was simply the lesser of two evils: the survey guy who won't take no for an answer, or me. I know what she's thinking; I know what you all think. None of you hide it that well, it's written all over your faces.

It still amazes me the effect I can have on people without doing anything. I can sit here on the busy street and there are two reactions that people have at the very sight of me. Some people will accidentally glance my way before realising what they are actually looking at and so will make a valiant effort not to look again for fear of being caught. When this occurs there is an awkwardness that settles between us; well, have you ever tried really hard not to look at something that you want to have another glance at? The other sorts of people are not so awkwardly English in their conduct; these people don't seem to care. They will stare without giving my feelings a second thought. To them I am not someone with feelings, I am a thing to be viewed, something medical science should be able to fix in this day and age.

Everyone has a story and everyone has problems. I am no different. I've always been this way, ever since I can remember. I don't consider myself to be normal, but nor am I abnormal. If I had the option, I would be 'normal', whatever that actually is. Throughout my life I have had numerous doctors' appointments and hospital procedures to correct the mark. My parents were adamant that whatever was offered to us was worth trying if there was the slightest chance it could have any effect. I don't believe the motivation for this had anything to do with having the perfect looking child; they simply wanted their daughter to have a chance in this world without her face affecting everything she did. At first, my doctor refused to do anything, insisting that the mark would simply fade after a couple of months. It didn't. My birthmark is what is called a port-wine stain; it is a result of blood vessels developing abnormally and the only treatment is laser therapy. I had nine of these treatments in the first decade of my life and although it was reduced, it didn't alter as much as my parents had hoped. By the time I reached my thirteenth birthday, I decided I'd had enough. There was no point persevering with the treatment that would only lead to disappointment. I know it hurt my parents to hear it, but I didn't need the treatment; when I look in the mirror I can see past the large red mark. My birthmark travels from my ear to my neck and covers most of my right cheek.

The reaction I get now is similar to the reaction I got at school. Although I wouldn't admit it to my parents, I was petrified when they dropped me off on my first day as a year seven at the local comprehensive. I wanted to prove to them and myself, that I *could* do this without the need for them to hold my hand. That very first day signified the reactions I was to endure from that day on. There was a split between the pupils and even some of the teachers; some just starred and sniggered with their friends as I walked past, whereas others made a valiant effort to see past it, but acted awkwardly around me for fear of saying or doing something wrong.

Before lessons even started, I was assigned to someone who was to look after me, Becca. We met in reception and were introduced to one another by the head mistress, who reiterated strict instructions to Becca to take care of me. Stepping out of reception I looked at my new 'friend'; she was taller than me and we looked very different. Apart from the obvious, she was blond with blue eyes whereas I have dark brown hair with eyes to match.

'What happened to your face?' From the off Becca wasn't backward in coming forward. As she asked she took a step closer to inspect the right side of my face.

'Don't know, it's just there…. has been since I was born'. She nodded and seemed satisfied with the answer. For the rest of the day the very sight of me was met with diverse reactions, but Becca didn't seem to notice either my face or even the other pupil's reactions. While I was at school, I was fortunate enough to have a group of school friends who really could see past my face and treat me normally, just like any other teenage girl. It was then that I felt as 'normal' as I ever have, so much so, that when others felt it necessary to ask or tease me about my face, I was only then reminded that I wasn't just like the rest of my friends. But from time to time, when people would let me, I could forget all about it.

When I was in my final year of school I was called to reception on the first day of the school year. On arrival I found two girls sitting outside the headmistress's office, one just gazed at the ground whilst, in contrast, the other seemed interested in all her new surroundings. Both were new year sevens, easily identified by their brand new clothes, which are usually on the large side, because 'they'll grow into it'. I entered Mrs Goodwin's office and sat in the chair while she finished her phone conversation.

'Hello Lorna, did you have a good summer?' I always liked our head teacher; her smile had such warmth to it.

'Yes, I had a great summer, thank you'

'Good. Lorna, I was wondering if you could do me a favour… no doubt you noticed the two girls sitting outside. One of them is Jemma James, the other is Kate Sawyer. Kate has a port-wine stain much like yourself…I have assigned Jemma to help her settle in, as Becca helped you when you first arrived. I was hoping that you would also help her. You have settled in so well and I think you would be a good role model for her.'

Upon leaving the office, Mrs Goodwin introduced the two girls to me. Jemma beamed up at me. She was obviously a confident out going girl, whereas Kate took her time to even look in my direction. Looking at the timid girl before me, it dawned on me that this is how I must have appeared, shy and awkward, on my first day. As Kate looked up I saw her birthmark, which was more central than my own, but slightly smaller. I crouched down so I was at eye level with Kate and tried to persuade her to go to class. With Jemma's help we encouraged the timid girl to go to class by explaining the fears I had on my first day; within ten minutes she walked off quite happily with her new friend.

I got to know Kate quite well during her time at the school and watched her develop into a confident teenager who would often give as good as she got if anyone dared to tease her. It was because of her that I really came to accept myself and the way I look. If other people can't see past it, that's *their* problem, not *mine*! To you, I represent something a bit scary. It would be easier for you if I didn't enter your safe, civilised, normal society. That way you could pretend people like me didn't exist; you wouldn't have to deal with us. Just get back to your carefree lives. I know this because I am like you and that fact is what really terrifies you. Next time you walk past me or someone else who does not look 'normal', who is not like you, just know, if the circumstances had been a little different, it could be you sitting here, looking like this, instead of me.

Part Four: Reflections on Learning

Tick, Tock

Gemma Pargeter

Tick, tock, tick, tock, tick, tock. The clock came down, the batteries came out. Drip, drip, drip, drip, drip. 'ENOUGH!!' The kitchen door was slammed shut behind a rather flustered looking girl, as she scurried off to her bedroom for some much needed silence. Time to concentrate, time to be creative, time to write a story. What a crazy idea, what had she let herself in for? She couldn't write a story! 'You can barely read a story, let alone write one!' her friend had chuckled on the bus earlier that week when realizing her predicament. It was common knowledge amongst her friends that she was not a literary type. She always judged a book by its cover and would only ever read trashy, 'chick lits' which would usually take her a good month to complete. The only experience the girl had was several years of writing academic essays, to which she had become accustomed. She had to smile as she found herself sitting cross-legged on her bed, longing for the simplicity of the structured essays that had once been loathed with a passion. Before her lay the infinity of story land and she knew there was only one thing for it; start reading stories.

Fascinated by her newfound knowledge, she now believed herself to be a true expert at all there was to know on the subject of death and disease, much to her family's dismay as they endured dinner after dinner of the symptoms of fatal diseases, along with all the gory details. Now was the time to take the plunge and begin her story.

What a fantastic feeling it was to hold the warm sheets as they were fed through the printer, containing the treasured words that she had pondered over for weeks. Who would have thought that so much knowledge could be contained in a few simple sentences that would have otherwise needed scrupulous referencing if in an essay? This was by far her most satisfying accomplishment this term and she was sure that it contained more information hidden within the text than any factual account could be capable of. Though her first story was finished, she knew her story writing days had only just begun.

Bibliography Story

Hannah Marie Davis

The girl sat hunched over her faded desk, looking despondently at her story, wondering how on earth she would even get a pass mark for the three thousand carefully crafted words which she had spent hours putting together until they flowed smoothly and neatly across her page. At first, the idea of being assessed through story telling, as opposed to the somewhat tedious essay format, had sent an excited shiver down her spine, yet, now she felt somewhat doomed. How could she demonstrate sociological knowledge through a creative writing task? How could she support and source her ideas? Then it dawned upon her, an annotated bibliography!

'An annotated bibliography? Ya what?' questioned her doubtful housemate whilst carefully manoeuvring a biscuit into a steaming mug of tea. 'Are you sure there's even a thing such as an annotated wodge-am-thingy? Even if there is, you'll have to include it into ya word count and then that won't leave ya much room for ya story telling will it now?' She slipped out of the room, steeling herself for not retorting at her nonchalant lump of a housemate. Sat back at her desk, accompanied by her own mug of steaming tea and plate of biscuits, she set to work. Underneath each book title in her bibliography, she wrote a few sentences describing what aspect of that particular reading had inspired her work and how she had utilised the knowledge that she had gained from it. Perfect. She finished long after her tea had gone cold but when she placed her final full stop on the page full of neat and tidy lines, she felt a sense of relief and achievement. She had a feeling that her 'annotated wodge-am-thingy' had the makings of a success!

Visual Sociology

Picturing the Social World

Phil Mizen and Carol Wolkowitz
Module Convenors

The rapid growth of Visual Sociology in the past 10 years shows increasing recognition of the importance of the visual in the construction of social institutions, social identities and social conflicts. The visual is as important to the way people give meaning to their everyday relationships (the family album, the holiday snap, the wedding video) as to their perception of world events, so it's no wonder that it has become a focus of interest for sociologists. Moreover, visual materials can also be used as the starting point for a range of research methods, for instance by providing opportunities for interacting with informants or for tracing visible evidence of social change in the appearance of different localities. New visual technologies have made it much easier and less expensive to adopt such visual methods. For instance, the disposable camera has made it more practicable to ask participants in sociological studies to show how they see things in a very immediate and convincing way, by taking pictures themselves and talking about them with researchers. Rapid advances in digital technology and the spread of home computing have, in the affluent world at least, changed significantly our capacity to make, exchange and display photographic images.

Our main aim in creating the new second year module in Visual Sociology was to enable students to become active researchers, producing knowledge of the social world through both pictures and words. Although visual sociology is rarely offered as a subject for undergraduates, their experience of using mobile phone cameras, digital camcorders and new online ways of displaying and sharing their snaps means that many students have more confidence than their elders when it comes to digital photography. Our new module seeks to build on and add to these skills, as well as introducing students to more analytical approaches to pictures and picture production. For simplicity's sake we decided to organise the course, at least to begin with, around digital still photography. We have, however, drawn on photography's rich history in lectures and seminars through, for instance, the socially engaged documentary photography produced by the likes of Sebastião Salgado, Walker Evans and Dorothea Lange and the writings and images of pioneers in the field of visual sociology, such as John Berger,

Jean Mohr and Howard Becker. Recent textbooks in visual sociology and anthropology by Caroline Knowles and Paul Sweetman, Sarah Pink, and Jon Prosser, along with the revamped journal *Visual Studies*, provide useful ways into examining the potential of photography as a means to explore social life, perhaps through 'photo-elicitation' techniques, photographic resurveys, visual ethnographies and the production of photographic diaries. Workshops held throughout the year enhance skills in producing, manipulating, storing and displaying images.

The seminars form a crucial part of the course. For instance, we started getting to know each other in the autumn by comparing the 'mug shots' on everyone's University ID cards with the photographs of ourselves as children. This produced interesting insights from the outset —about the varied purposes to which photography is put, for instance and the ways in which these purposes are reflected in the kinds of images produced. The wide age-range of students and tutors meant that we could also begin to think about changing photographic technologies, from black-and-white to colour, from matte to glossy, and changing conventions for picturing children and families.

Later on in term one we asked students to go out into the field and undertake a photographic survey of one kind of work and to analyse the results sociologically. Their presentations ranged widely, including studies of a local abattoir, a high street clothes chain, a taxi rank, 'outside' manual labour, bar and service workers and the embodied intellectual labour of fellow students in the university library. The photographs they took and projected in class captured aspects of social life vividly and succinctly. Still photography seems to hold the flux of the social world still, just for an instant and discussing what one can see as a result, encourages new conversations between all of us involved in the module.

Importantly, the module offers many students their first significant experience of doing research and they were very appreciative of each other's efforts. Taking pictures led to close and systematic observations of the social world and encouraged students to be reflexive about the social interactions producing the images had involved. The Modern Records Centre on campus provided an opportunity for students to examine photographs in its collections as historical documents, including the BP archives, giving them practice in relating the content of images to the historical contexts in which they are produced and used. Such considerations were again to the fore when we considered the Abu Ghraib photographs in spring term. With the submission of students' final projects at the end of the year, we were very impressed by their ability to use still photography analytically and their sensitivity to the moral and ethical implications of using photographic material in social research. For us as tutors, the data they presented — through lively colour photographs — made a dramatic and exciting change from the usual exam scripts and conventional essays.

One might well ask whether photographs are valid as a source of data or evidence. The answer is yes, but only when they are interpreted within an understanding of the context in which they are produced and viewed. In its awareness that there are different ways of picturing the social world, visual sociology is no different from other qualitative methods; indeed one of its benefits is that it keeps reminding us that information about the social world is inevitably shaped by the research methods adopted.

Key texts

Berger, J. and Mohr, J. (1975) *A Seventh Man: A Book of Images and Words about the Experience of Migrant Workers* Harmonsworth: Penguin.

Knowles, C. and Sweetman, P. (Eds). (2004) *Picturing the Social Landscape* London: Routledge.

Lister, M. (1995) *The Photographic Image in Digital Culture* London: Routledge.

Pink, S. (2001) *Doing Visual Ethnography* London: Sage.

Prosser, J., (Ed). (1998) *Image-Based Research: A Source Book for Qualitative Researchers* London: Routledge Falmer.

Rose, Gillian. (2003) 'Family Photographs and Domestic Spacings: A Case Study' *Transactions of the Institute of British Geographers* 28(1):1-18.

Salgado, Sebastião. (1993) *Workers: An Archaeology of the Industrial Age* London: Phaidon.

Sontag, Susan. (1971) *On Photography* London: Penguin.

Part One: Picturing the Social World

Visual Representations of Contemporary Intellectual Labour

EmmaVryenhoef

Manual labour has been widely depicted through visual methods, but academics often neglect to observe their own work and environment. This research uses the representation of a library in order to investigate how useful visual methods can be in capturing what is intellectual labour. This project examines the position of intellectual work within wider views on labour and representations of the body. It locates the problematic nature of the intellectual as part of mind/body and gender dichotomies and looks at how this is neutralised through social and spatial controls.

Wolkowitz's article, *The Working Body as Sign* (2001), uses the example of photographs by L. Hine which encompass pictures of home working and the construction of the Empire State Building to illustrate how 'the construction of masculine and female bodies takes place in relation to work as much as other areas of social life'. The themes identified here of the gendering and sexualising of work are part of the context within which intellectual work exists. Morgan's (1993) article clarifies the position of the intellectual within this framework. Locating it in the realm of the masculine/rational rather than the feminine/physical. Given this contradiction of the active aspect of the masculine ideal with the passivity of 'thinking', how is intellectual work embodied to be compatible with this? Are these dichotomies about work propagated or subverted?

Taking into account these concepts, Goffman's (1967) theories on impression management and social roles become highly relevant, especially in regards to the use of props and tools in order to create an appropriate representation of work depending on the situation. How then does social space facilitate this embodiment? Is it another more permanent prop, a form of sustaining ideals about the embodiment of work through people as social agents interacting with it?

Tim Strangleman's (2004) article critiquing the absence of visual methods in exploring work within the journal, *Work, Employment and Society*, emphasised for me the great interest academics have in exploring the 'opposite' to their own work, in some ways contributing to the view of manual labour as belonging to the 'other', it also indicated a distinct lack of interest in conceptualising intellectual work. Given the problematic power relations involved in photography, is it actually possible to picture the work of others without misinterpreting it or creating a ridged subject/object dichotomy?

Methodology

The photography took place in Coventry University's Lancaster library on a weekday afternoon during the third term of the academic year. This was after several previous visits to the building in order to familiarise myself with the location, ensure that a productive level of access could be gained and to determine its suitability to the research questions outlined in the review of the substantive literature. I remained on the second floor of the building and tried to capture the different areas used for study. Within this generalisation, I narrowed in on any specific sites of interest that I discovered and collected other visual resources I could find both during and after the fieldwork, the Internet was especially helpful in this aspect of the project.

Access was hard to gain and it was dependent upon my agreement to abide by certain regulations, this aspect most shaped and restricted the possibilities for the use of visual methods. Access was granted on the condition that I spent no more than 20 minutes taking photographs, that staff and students should not be pictured unless asked and that, if possible, I should refrain from picturing students altogether to avoid disturbing them. Due to the nature of the constraints placed upon conducting research in the location of the library, locating the methodology primarily around shooting scripts and grounded theory (Suchar 1997) became invaluable in organising the process of photography. Also, although it was not actively discouraged, it was mentioned that I might wish to avoid the third floor as, 'it was quite a different layout due to the university running out of funding,' this attempt to further control the research drew the feasibility of the study into question, especially combined with the precarious nature of further access should I continue. However, it raised interesting tensions between, what I had previously believed to be an open public setting, which was now being defended as though it were a private one.

Unable to conduct photo-elicitation or a restudy, my focal point, because of these regulations, became about spatial usage and the way in which the library was interacted with. Already, what had been taken for granted as a public situation, was actually a very controlled and private one, revealed just through issues and stipulations around gaining admission. These photographs are an effort to picture the library as a social space, with both its public and private aspects.

With the possibilities for fieldwork already narrowed I was acutely aware of how my presence, once I had gained access, affected the behaviour of those working in the area I chose to concentrate upon. I became an object of intense curiosity since my conduct was alien in that environment, however, explaining that I was also a student meant that some people were willing to participate and it earned me a few photographs. Despite sharing this status, I was still aware that I was out of place, using the digital camera, this was unavoidable, yet it clearly marked out that I was there in a very different capacity. Although I could have used a camera phone in order to be more inconspicuous and unobtrusive, that technology was not available and I feel that the quality of these digital images speaks for itself during analysis. The covert aspect of the camera phone, I believe, would have also been problematic for library staff and may have made it more difficult to gain access, due to the concealed nature of the device. The camera was definitely detrimental to securing access. The fact that the library staff requested an electronic copy of the photographs rather than the whole assignment indicates a need to control the visual imagery that represents the library and shows the importance with which people view photographs, seeing them as conveyors of a transcendent truth.

I informed the staff of the nature of the research I was doing, explaining that the focal point was the use and categorisation of space and how people interacted with it. Some of the stipulations for access complied with my own intentions to keep the people depicted in the photographs anonymous. However, on searching for visual materials to accompany my photographs, it became apparent that these restrictions did not apply to the university's own publicity of the library. A search for online photographs revealed many images in which there was enough detail for students to be identified. They portrayed what I interpret as a busy environment, propagating an image of efficiency and work. This went some way to counteract my ethical concerns, indicating that perhaps I was overestimating the disturbing effect my presence would have. However, despite the fact that the ethical concerns of the library staff do not necessarily seem to be concordant with the welfare of students and possible participants in the study, that still does not negate my own ethical issues and responsibilities in relation to the students.

I limited the time and number of photos I took, in an effort to minimise my presence. Where appropriate, I explained why I was there and if people were identifiable in the photos I asked the permission of the participants to use the image. As touched upon earlier, the restrictions placed on the study in order to gain access to this location, severely limited the opportunity for active participation by library users. Although photography was invaluable

in picturing this social setting and it uncovered a lot about the way the spatial organisation and furniture affects the study environment and bodies at work, in some ways it also neglects the viewpoint of library users and colludes in the passive portrayal of intellectual labour.

Space and the Body

This photograph (Figure 1) shows four types of spatial usage, the corridor areas generated by the position of shelves and desks, the bookshelves themselves and the more public computing area in comparison to the private carrels for study. The carrels are organised around the edge of the room and the bookshelves are placed to separate this quiet area from the rest of the library's occupants. The computer desks also have ergonomic grooves, fashioned in them to create a more individual workspace. The chairs facilitate working in a certain upright position; they are clearly not for 'lounging' upon. With the exception of the person standing, who was just leaving the area, all the bodies in this picture display a commonality. They occupy a specific space in a specific manner, the space is defined by the furniture and equipment they use, which is positioned by the library and the manner is that of 'concentration', heads lowered, arms and legs pulled in.

This 'thinking' position is taken up regardless on age, gender, or race. However, the state of intellectual work which they embody can be argued as a gendered, classed and racialised one. As Lutz and Collins describe in their content analysis of National Geographic, 'deeply ingrained notions of racial hierarchy make it seem more 'natural' for dark-skinned people to be at work and engaged in strenuous activity (Lutz & Collins 1993; p.162) And in terms of gender Morgan emphasises the position of thinking and its belonging in the rational realms of masculinity:

> 'Insofar as intellectual labour is woven into wider patterns of
> the sexual division of labour, then to do thinking is to occupy
> a particularly distinctive and often privileged place in space,
> public or private. The thinker allows for no interruptions from
> the mundane world of domestic responsibilities or small
> children. Yet obligations are placed upon the thinker to be seen
> doing thinking, to occupy space in a particular watchful or
> concentrating manner.'

Therefore we propagate images, ideas and bodily interactions which are based on our assumptions and expectations about work.

With the changes in the sexual division of labour this has become more problematic in contemporary society and thus the ways in which we embody and perform thinking seek to legitimate the nature of intellectual work and its position. Performing 'thinking' seeks to transcend notions of racism and sexism but it does so by integrating nonconformist bodies and therefore reproducing social paradigms. The body is an entity upon which anxieties about the validity of intellectual work can be placated. It is arguable that because of this, rational, intellectual work is just as embodied as manual labour. Failure to recognise the embodied quality of intellectual work is due to the dichotomies that surround mind and body, constructing the mind as within but not part of the body, creating an abstract entity (Morgan 1993). This is compounded by the association of the body and work with physical action. This inadequacy of intellectual work is off set through validation by physically demonstrating thinking as behaviour. The use of props such as pens, glasses, books, even a bottle of water indicating endurance and fasting according to library rules, all help to 'legitimate the title of thinker' (Morgan 1993; Goffman 1967).

As discussed, the space of the library requires a particular kind of bodily conduct, which is under the scrutiny of staff, the university and other students represented by the Students Union. In Figure 3 the final line of this poster reads, 'Library rules are for the benefit of all our users. People who break the rules will be asked to leave and sanctions applied. Coventry University Students' Union fully supports these rules on behaviour in the University Library.' This 'internalisation' of university rules is via the support of the student body's political representative, the Union, thus generating the idea of self-regulation and surveillance as a way of policing this social setting (Rabinow 1984).

Figure 1

Figure 2

Figure 3

The Individual and The Systematic

The photographs on the following pages show a stark contrast between two different areas and uses of space. Figure 4 pictures a computer area with a large window, enabling students to look out onto other sections of the library and the university campus. The glossy magazine on the desk is not an object usually symbolic of work. These computers are on a straight desk; the space is far more open than in previous photographs, there are no dividers up between them. Technology, in this case, seems to be viewed as a tool rather than a producer of knowledge.

In contrast, the windows in Figure 5 are blocked out by the sides of the booths, this affords the occupants no other immediate view than the desk and its surrounding wooden walls. In this sense, the inhabitation of a defined space is enforced, there are limited distractions and interruptions from other people. One student observed on seeing the photographs that he 'didn't realise how high the ceilings were' and that it was 'very white'. This decor is void of distractions and is symbolic of the idea that thinking is a product of an individual mind. The body positions in Photo 5 are similar to those described in the previous paragraph. There are more computer workstations on the left hand side and a group study table in the background, which illustrates the defined nature of the space.

Although thinking is identified with individual ingenuity, there is a tension in this image between the aforementioned ideology and the systematic large-scale layout of identical carrels. The mass production of intellectual knowledge and the commoditisation of learning that exists in education is reflected in the utilisation of the library as a social space which is poised on the borderline between the public and private.

Figure 4

Figure 5

Form and Content

Difficulties over access and research into other visual resources depicting the library revealed the double standard involved in ensuring a positive image of the facility is promoted. The layout ensures correct embodiment of work by using the space to discipline bodies and although the library is a public space, admittance is controlled and dependant upon membership to the university or plausible reasoning for use, in other words, it is arbitrary. The privacy of the library conceals the problematic inactivity of thinking, which is so opposed to traditional mainstream representations of work; however, it simultaneously uses this 'inactivity', or more accurately embodiment, of intellectual labour to measure its effectiveness. The contradiction lies in the fact that the form, (the structure and look of the space and how it is interacted with) rather than the content (the quality of learning that students experience) is taken as an indicator of success. This highlights the importance of the visual when policing (Sontag 1979) the library as a space and assessing its success and usefulness as a study area; it is also illustrative of the power of visual methods in portrayal more generally.

There should be concern about viewing these images within a wider cultural context that sees photography as an objective source, as the ultimate tool of lasting visual evidence. The Library defines and uses photography in a specific way, as do all social agents and entities that deploy it as a tool. Photography's 'status as a technology varies with the power relations which invest it. Its nature as a practice depends upon the institutions and agents which define it and set it to work' (Tagg 1997). Given the importance of the visual in validating the library as a study area and legitimising intellectual work, the problem with these images is that, although through analysis they go some way to subverting dichotomies about the body and work, alone they collude with the passive representation of intellectual labour. Even through analysis, the people in these photographs become 'subjected to a scrutinizing gaze,' (Tagg 1988) it just originates from a different context. It is easy to see this social space as part of a wider capitalist culture, however, in doing so, we too negate individual experiences of learning, therefore risking conforming to the examination of only the form of social space.

In conclusion, dichotomies about the mind/body are propagated on the surface of intellectual labour, however, representations of intellectual work are arguably just as embodied as those of manual labour. This is due to the perceived inactivity of thinking, which therefore requires that intellectual work be rigorously demonstrated in an appropriate manner, a practice that is

aided and controlled through the use of permanent spatial features as props. In terms of methodology, using straight visual methods is extremely problematic as it conforms to the view of the worker as subject and fits into the wider framework of the visual as surveillance, only picturing the form of social life within its setting, rather than examining the effect of different sites of production and viewing (Rose 2001). If problems of access could be overcome, the use of photo-elicitation would be far more beneficial in creating a picture of how and why intellectual work takes place and how the space in which it occurs impacts upon and reflects its nature.

Bibliography

Goffman, E. (1967) *Interaction Ritual,* New York: Doubleday Anchor.

Hammersely, M. & Atkinson, P. (1989) *Ethnography: principles in practice,* London: Routledge.

Knowles, C. & Sweetman, P. (eds.), (2004) *Picturing the Social Landscape: Visual Methods and the Sociological Imagination,* London: Routledge.

Morgan, D. (1993) 'You Too Can Have a Body Like Mine: Reflections on the Male Body and Masculinities,' in Scott, S. & Morgan, D. (eds.) *Body Matters,* London: Falmer.

Lutz, C. A. & Collins, J. L. (1993) *Reading National Geographic*, Chicago: University of Chicago Press

Rabinow, P. (1984) *The Foucault Reader,* London: Penguin.

Prosser, J. & Schwartz, D. (1998) 'Photographs within the Sociological Research Process,' in Prosser, J. (ed.), *Image-Based Research,* London: Falmer.

Rose, G. (2001) *Visual Methodologies,* London: Sage.

Sontag, S. (1979) *On Photography,* Harmondsworth: Penguin.

Suchar, C. S. (1997) 'Grounding Visual Sociology Research in Shooting Scripts,' *Qualitative Sociology,* 20(1): 33-55.

Strangleman, T. (2004) 'Ways of (not) seeing work: The visual as a blind spot in WES?' *Work, Employment and Society,* 18(1): 179-192.

Tagg, J. (1988) *The Burden of Representation,* Basingstoke: Macmillan.

Tagg, J. (1997) 'Evidence, Truth and Order; Photographic Records and the Growth of the State' in Wells, L. (ed.), *Photography; a critical introduction,* London: Routledge.

Wolkowitz, C. (2001) 'The Working Body as Sign: Historical Snapshots' in Backett-Milburn, K. & McKie, L. (eds.), *Constructing Gendered Bodies,* Basingstoke: Palgrave.

Seeing behind closed doors: A visual study of power and pride in an abattoir

Naomi Alsop

The gendered aspects of meat eating and to a lesser extent, meat production, have become the focus of much vegetarian and feminist sociological analysis since the 1990s. Traditionally, meat eating and production have been associated with men; man is the hunter, woman the gatherer. Indeed meat eating is so intertwined with masculinity (Sobal 2005: 137) that for a man to become vegetarian is to '[C]hallenge an essential part of the masculine role' (Adams 1990: 49). Moreover, the masculine nature of meat-eating is extended and magnified in the abattoir. This study will look at two aspects of the power relations within a small family-owned abattoir: patriarchal power and the relationship between the slaughterhouse worker and the changing nature of the animal product.

The nature of man's relationship with animals can be seen in the power which men exert over animals. For Berger the zoos of the 18th and 19th centuries represented early colonial power through the capture of wild animals from exotic countries (1980: 19). For Fiddes, 'Consuming the muscle flesh of other highly evolved animals is a statement of extreme power' (1991: 2). Indeed, Adams argues that the power that men exert over animals through slaughtering animals and the consumption of meat is analogous to the power they exert over women (1990: 54). Moreover, Adams identifies knives as 'enabling mechanisms' for the render of 'living animal into edible dead flesh' and cites them as an important aspect of the violence which occurs within the slaughterhouse (1990: 50). She argues that both animals and women experience being objectified, fragmented, transformed into a consumable and denied as a being: '[T]o feel like a piece of meat is to be treated like an inert object when one is (or was) in fact a living, feeling being' (ibid). Thus animals are subject to the same patriarchal subjugation as women.

The patriarchal nature of the power balance within the slaughterhouse creates a highly masculine environment. In her study into the employment of women within the meat industry, Leisk found that there was opposition from male slaughterhouse operators to working with women: '[T]he presence of women was thought to affect the masculine environment, so that men were inhibited about swearing and behaving as they normally would in an all-male workplace' (2000: 168). Thus women were often excluded from working in the slaughterhouse despite expressing a desire to do such work (ibid: 169).

Whilst women are often excluded from working in the slaughterhouse due to the masculine environment, wider society chooses to be excluded. Fiddes (1991: 100) argues that the process of slaughtering is designed to disguise the animal origins of the meat and produce a fragmented product which bears no similarity to the appearance of the original animal. Thus, in its fragmentation, the animal becomes an absent referent (Adams 1990) and the meat eater is able to distance him or herself from the origins of meat. The dislike of being reminded that meat is the produce of an animal results in the slaughterhouse and its workers being marginalised and excluded from mainstream society (Fiddes 1991: 83).

Methodology
This study examines the working environment of a small, family owned abattoir, using visual methods. It follows the workers' interactions both with their environment and with the changing forms of the product. The research employed the following methodologies in the study of the abattoir: photo-analysis, three unstructured photo-elicitation interviews with Henry Moore, the owner of the business, informal interviews with Henry and the slaughtermen and a photo-elicitation with the slaughtermen. The research was conducted over a seven month period, from November 2005 to June 2006 and involved several visits to the slaughterhouse.

Adams wrote that 'Generally if we enter a slaughterhouse we do so through the writings of someone else who has entered for us' (1990: 51). The difficulty with relying on the written word to understand the slaughterhouse is that language is liable to either sensationalise the process of meat production or reduce it to technical jargon. My instinct as a meat-eater is to use language as free of emotion as possible, possibly to assuage any feelings of guilt I might be suppressing rather than to reflect my experience within the slaughterhouse. If I were to use personal language I might begin to anthropomorphise the animal, thus making my presence in the slaughterhouse more difficult. The inclusion of photographs within this project acts as evidence which can be interpreted in light of the reader's biases rather than mine alone. As Back wrote, '[O]ne of the great advantages of photography is that photographs need – in one sense – simply to be shown rather than explicated' (2004: 135). However, it should be noted that the photographs are my interpretation of the slaughterhouse. Just as the written word can have implicit biases, so too can the image.

Images of slaughterhouses are comparatively rare, perhaps due to society's desire to absent the referent within meat eating. Those images that do exist are often from a vegetarian perspective and show industry worst practice in large industrial scale abattoirs. This study was conducted in a small family owned abattoir which prides itself on operating 'best practice', as Henry Moore put it. Thus in this instance the inclusion of visual imagery acts as an important counterbalance to the images of slaughterhouses that may have been seen elsewhere.

Access and ethical considerations
Access to the abattoir was gained through my brother-in-law, Henry Moore, joint owner of the business. He supervised all of my visits due to the potentially dangerous nature of the environment. Thus the photographs I made were dictated to a large extent by where it was safe for me to stand and possibly by the presence of the business owner.

Ethical research is important in any study. However, there was one significant ethical consideration which I did not identify before the study: the effect that being in the slaughterhouse environment would have on me. As a meat eater I had approached the study with the attitude that if I can eat meat I should be able to cope with seeing how an animal is killed. Yet despite entering the abattoir with a deliberately matter-of-fact approach there were moments when I was taken aback by my reaction to the process. For example, I was aware of a difficult symbolism in the dead pigs apparently staring at their reflection in pools of their own blood, with their internal organs hanging feet away from them (figure 1). Moreover, I found the moment of 'sticking' or cutting the throat difficult and dealt with it by concentrating on composing and framing images within the camera (figure 2). However, the biggest difficulty I found was not due to any anthropomorphisation of the animals, which I had identified as a possibility before the study. Instead the difficulty arose by me relating my body to the pigs. For about a week after my initial trip round the slaughterhouse my flesh appeared too similar to the pigs and my mind repeatedly imposed the sight of the pigs' entrails onto my body (figure 3). I had read Adam's analogy of the treatment of animals and women, but I had not anticipated such bodily identification with the animals.

Figure 1 (above): Slaughtered pigs stare into their reflections in pools of their own blood a few feet away from their internal organs. Naomi Alsop, November 2005.

Figure 2 (left): The slaughterman 'sticking' the pig. After the pig has been drained of blood it will be scalded and dehaired before it has its internal organs removed and its body split in-two. Naomi Alsop, November 2005.

Figure 3 (above right): the pig is rinsed to remove any debris from the dehairing process before its internal organs are removed. Naomi Alsop, November 2005.

The distorting effect of my presence in the slaughterhouse

Initially it had been my intention to use my own photographs throughout the study. However, after my first visit to the abattoir, I became aware that my presence as a stranger and a young woman, might be having a distorting effect on the behaviour within the slaughterhouse. One image (figure 4) particularly underlined my suspicion. I was aware that one of the men I was photographing (Brian, pseudonym) had become very self-conscious where previously he had not been. Henry explained afterwards that at the moment I had made the photograph Brian had been cutting the anus out of the pig. I suspect that as a woman, my presence had made him more aware of the connotations his actions may carry than if I had been a man. I therefore redesigned my research to incorporate photographs made by Henry so I could see his perspective on the abattoir. Figure 5 justified my decision to withdraw from the photography of the slaughterhouse. The picture shows Brian and Alex (pseudonym) laughing as Brian sharpens a knife (a symbol invested with much masculine pride within the abattoir, as will be discussed). When I asked Henry if he could remember what they were laughing about when he had taken the picture there was a long pause before he answered: 'There were a few references to you, I think. Which is typical slaughterman, I'm afraid. You know, we're just a randy group.'

Henry's observation of the slaughterhouse workers was confirmation of an experience I had had a couple of days prior to the interview. I had gone to the business's premises to collect my camera after Henry had called unexpectedly to say his photographs were ready. Whereas previously I had taken care to dress conservatively, that day I did not have an opportunity to change my clothes and therefore was more casually dressed than I would have chosen. Consequently I became aware of a different atmosphere in the environment and some gestures were made about me. As the gestures and comments were made I was surprised to find I again identified with the pigs. I felt as if I had been reduced from a human being to my constituent parts. I had been transformed from woman to breasts, legs and bottom, just as the pigs were transformed from pig to loin, chops and fillet.

Figure 4 (left): My presence makes Brian self-conscious despite having removed a pig's anus hundreds of times before. Naomi Alsop, November 2005.

Figure 5 (below): Brian and Alex share a joke about me whilst Brian sharpens his knife. The knife is a symbol of masculine pride within the slaughter environment and much importance is attached to the ability to sharpen it well. The masculine pride taken in knives within the slaughterhouse may be indicative of a phallic symbolism. Henry Moore, June 2006.

The worker/animal relationship

In the photo-elicitation interviews conducted with Henry Moore, the relationship of the animal with the workers was a constant theme. The responses he gave to the images showed a dichotomy between the animal as product and being. In discussing figure 6, Henry explained why he had made the image by saying 'He was having a look at me, so I thought 'I'm going to take a photo of you." The power within the interaction that Henry describes lies with him: he owns both the right to look and the image of the animal, just as he owns the meat product which the animal will become. The pig looked at him in that moment and Henry responded by photographing the pig, thus enabling him to look at the pig later. Yet, at the same time, when Henry expresses his thoughts as a statement directed at the pig, he is acknowledging the pig as a being with the ability to look.

For Henry one of the most important aspects of his work was that the animals were respected. He described figure 7 as 'fairly useful' for its ability to show that the process of slaughtering is 'not as gory as people think […] not as horrendous as peoples' preconceptions of it are, you know. As long as it's done properly.' He went on to describe people's misconceptions of the process:

> *Because animals are being killed, people have this idea that something cruel is being done. I mean all right, ultimately an animal is dying, I mean nobody is going to try and deny that. I mean that puts meat on the plate, you know. But it's done in as humane, and, how can I put it? Almost as respectful a way as possible. […] if me dad left a little bit of fat on the side of his plate me granddad would say 'you eat that out of respect for the animal'. And I thought, brilliant, and what a lovely way of looking at things.[…] respect is a big thing.*

For Henry then, not absenting the animal referent is an important aspect of respecting the animal. His grandfather founded the business that Henry now owns with his brother and the sense of respecting the animal and acknowledging the sacrifice it made (however unintentional on the animal's part) has been handed down through the generations.

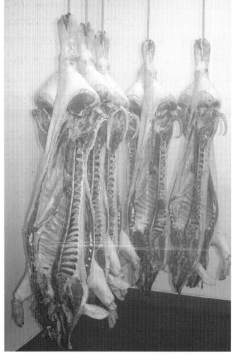

Figure 6 (above): The 'before' shot. The pigs in this image were described by Henry as being in their 'ante-mortem' state. Henry made the photograph as a reaction to the pig looking at him (June 2006).

Figure 7 (left): Henry made this image to show that the slaughter process is 'not as gory as people think'. Henry Moore, June 2006.

My experience in the slaughterhouse also emphasised the importance the workers placed on respect for the animals. For example, figure 9 shows Bert (pseudonym), one of the slaughterhouse workers 'dehairing' a dead pig; a careful operation. Bert was working on the pig's face as I photographed him and the process reminded me of a barber carefully shaving a client. Such care may have been due to a desire not to break the skin of the pig for aesthetic or regulatory reasons. However, the impression given was one of great care and respect for the animal. The carcass went on from there to have its internal organs removed and be split in half with a saw.

The masculine nature of the environment and implements
The masculine nature of the environment was also a recurrent theme, within which implements played an important role. When Henry was looking at figure 10 the focus of the picture, the knives in the scabbard, prompted me to ask the question 'Are knives important?' Henry immediately identified the knives and the worker's interactions with them as being 'macho':

> *There is a pride thing in having a sharp knife. It's probably a macho thing, I don't know 'cause I don't know many women slaughtermen, or slaughterwomen. Well I know of one. I don't actually know her, but knew of one slaughterhouse that had an actual female slaughterman [...] But particularly with slaughtermen it is a thing of sharpening your knives. [...] if you can sharpen a knife, as you've seen, and you can shave with it, you think phew [smiles and makes a gesture of perfection]. And, you know, it's very probably a man thing, a macho thing. And I can't explain it. [...] it's very much a pride thing.*

The association of knives, the enablers of violence within the slaughterhouse (Adams 1990: 50), with masculinity may be indicative of the power relations within the slaughterhouse. Henry's pictures show two images of slaughtermen sharpening their knives (figures 5 and 11).

Henry also identified figure 12 with masculinity. 'Again, a bit of a macho thing, if you notice on his knife scabbard, there, no real need for that, but I don't know if you know what that is? It's a bull ring. [...] it's a bit like a badge.' Thus the props of the slaughterhouse were associated with a masculine pride in the work being done and the men's ability to do it.

Figure 8 (above): Necessary signs. Regulations do not dictate the presence of the signs, but Henry feels they are necessary to reinforce that the welfare of the animal is paramount. Such reminders, he feels, would not have been necessary years ago. Henry Moore, June 2006 .

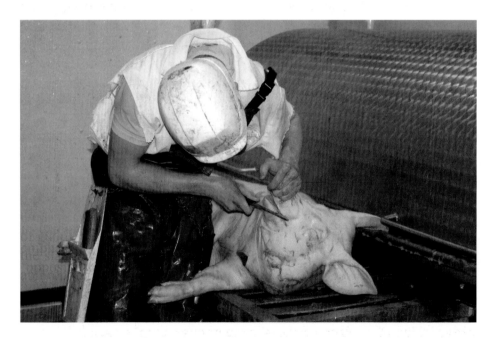

Figure 9 (above): After being scalded and mechanically dehaired, the process of dehairing is carefully finished off by hand in such a way it that brings to mind a barber shaving a client. Naomi Alsop, November 2005.

Henry associated the environment with the perception of butchers as womanisers. Upon Henry describing figure 5 as showing that slaughtermen were a 'randy group', I asked him if that was because the slaughter environment was very macho, which he answered it was. I then asked him if he could imagine a woman working in the slaughterhouse.

> *I could imagine a woman working in the slaughterhouse, but in this day and age. A generation ago, no. […] Yeah, a woman could go in there, and I don't think it would be very different because of the way a lot of women are nowadays, which I find very sad. Because I find so many women now will use bad language, as an instance. […] There are women who could do it, there are women who could do it very well, but it's not really a woman's environment.*

Conclusion

The photographs made in the process of this research showed four aspects of the slaughterhouse environment and the slaughterhouse workers, as discussed. First, they underlined the disruptive effect that my presence had upon the environment and the workers. Second, they were evidence, in conjunction with the photo-elicitation, that the animal is not an absent referent in the slaughterhouse to the degree suggested by Adams and Fiddes. Third, they showed the importance of respecting the animals and the pride which the workers derive from that. Fourth, they were evidence of the highly masculinised nature of the environment and the implements that were used in the slaughter process. The images were crucial to the discussion of the process in an abstract way within the photo-elicitation and often acted as a means of discovering 'unexpected significance in what is often only taken for granted' (Grady and Mechling 2003: 94). Future research into the difference in attitudes and differences in gendering between large industrial scale abattoirs and their smaller independent counterparts would be valuable.

For me, this study has changed both my approach to meat-eating and my patterns of consumption. I still eat meat, but I have come to value it more because the animal referent is no longer absent. Moreover, I no longer buy meat that has been produced in large abattoirs such as those shown in vegetarian literature. Instead I buy meat from small independent abattoirs, where pride in the job comes from the respect given to the animals.

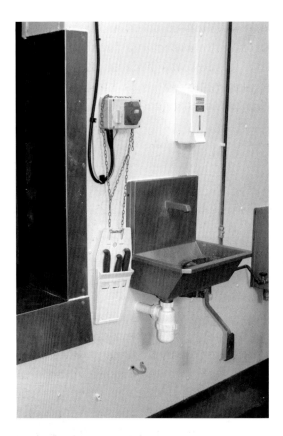

Figure 10 (left): Macho knives. The workers get a 'macho' pride from being able to maintain knives sharp enough to shave with. In response to the question 'Are knives important?' Henry answered 'I didn't take it for that reason, but now you've brought that up, yes, they are very important.' Henry Moore, June 2006.

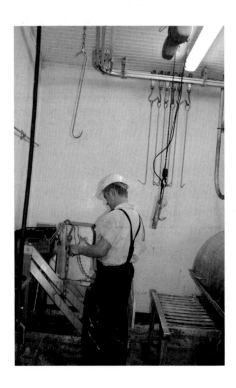

Figure 11 (left): Bert sharpens his knife. Henry Moore, June 2006.

Figure 12 (below): 'A macho thing'. Brian uses a bullring to attach his knife scabbard to his belt. Henry Moore, June 2006.

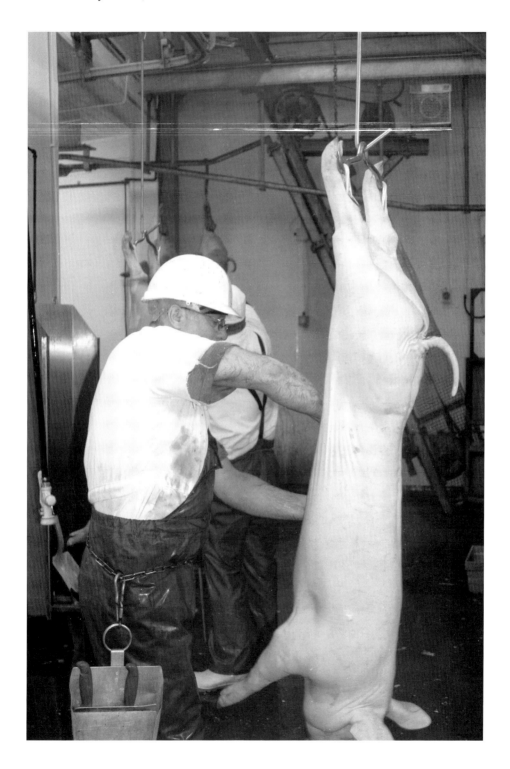

Bibliography

Adams, C. (1990) *The Sexual Politics of Meat*, Cambridge: Polity Press.

Back, L. (2004) 'Listening with our eyes' in Knowles, C. and Sweetman, P. *Picturing the Social Landscape*, London: Routledge.

Baker, S. (1993) *Picturing the Beast: Animals, Identity and Representation*, Manchester: Manchester University Press.

Berger, J. (1980) 'Why look at animals?' in *About Looking*, London: Writers and Readers Publishing Cooperative.

Coe, S. (1995) *Dead Meat,* New York: Four Walls Eight Windows.

Donnellan, C (Ed.) (1996) *Meat-eaters Versus Vegetarians*, Cambridge: Independence.

Fiddes, N. (1991) *Meat: A Natural Symbol,* London: Routledge.

Grady, J. and Mechling, J. (2003) 'Editors introduction: Putting animals in the picture', *Visual Studies,* 18(2): 92-95.

Harper, D. (2002) 'Talking about pictures: a case for photo-elicitation', *Visual Studies,* 17(1): 13-26.

Holm, L. and Mohl, M. (2000) 'The role of meat in everyday food culture: an analysis of an interview study in Copenhagen', *Appetite,* 34: 277-283.

Konecki, K.T. (2005) 'The problem of symbolic interaction and of constructing self', *Qualitative Sociology Review,* 1(1): 68-89.

Leisk, H. (2000) *The Employment of Women in the British Meat Industry.* Unpublished thesis submitted at the University of Warwick.

Levi Martin, J. (2000) 'What do animals do all day?: The division of labour, class bodies, and totemic thinking in the popular imagination', *Poetics,* 27: 195-231.

North, R. (1993) *Death by Regulation: The Butchery of the British Meat Industry,* London: IEA Health and Welfare Unit.

PETA. (2006) 'Meet your meat; *GotVeg.com,* accessed 5th June 2006', http://www.goveg.com/factoryfarming.asp

Pidgeon, M.E. (1932) *The Employment of Women in Slaughtering and Meat Packing,* Washington, USA: United States Government Printing Office.

Salgado, S. (1993) *Workers: An archaeology of the industrial age,* London: Phaidon.

Smith, M. (2002) 'The 'ethical' space of the abattoir: On the (in)human(e) slaughter of other animals', *Human Ecology Forum,* 9(2): 49-58.

Sobal, J. (2005) 'Men, meat and marriage: models of masculinity', *Food and Foodways,* 13: 135-158.

Suchar, C.S. (1997) 'Grounding Visual Sociology Research in Shooting Scripts', *Qualitative Sociology,* 20(1): 33-55.

Jillian: A Photo-elicitation

Steve Birks

The structure of this report will be created by the practical process of planning, developing and conducting a photo elicitation exercise and of the data analysis that follows. Harper, (2002) defines this process of photo elicitation as an event that uses visual images in structured or unstructured interviews. During the course of the assignment, consideration will be given to the claims that the process vigorously stimulates the memories of those involved and the intensity of the 'conversation ' (Banks, 2005). A process that Harper (2002) claims, gives the opportunity to produce 'rich and thick' descriptions of the social world, producing data that is highly valued by qualitative researchers.

If, as Harper (2002) states, photo elicitation interviews connect 'core definitions of the 'self' to society, culture and history' (p 14), it follows that the use of family archives as a source of images is appropriate, as they are closely connected with the identity of the family and the individual 'self ' (Chalfont, 1998). By focusing on a single individual and the positioning of 'self identification' in relationship to images from the family archive, it may be possible to generalise on the role of the family archives in the construction of the identity of the 'self' in relation to society in general. To access this information, Collier and Collier, (1986) propose that photo elicitation requires a triangular relationship between the researched, the researcher and the photographs that is a mutually beneficial relationship for the interpretation of knowledge.

Having ascertained the practical needs of a photo-elicitation, the existence of a family archive exists with the interviewee. It was possible on this basis, to approach an acquaintance. I have known Jillian (born in the 1930s) in a professional capacity through work for eighteen months, therefore I know only a little of her past and present life and no intimate details of her background and family.

After giving her a simple outline of photo elicitation, I asked for no preparation to be made, other than to have available the archive in whatever form it was stored in. This was on the understanding that an unstructured elicitation would permit Jillian to structure the elicitation around the areas she considered to be most significant; but that it could be focused by the interviewer in the desired areas, as is made clear by Schwartz (1992) who stated that 'if topics were raised that required clarification,' (p 11) the researcher may 'probe for further explanation' thereby focusing the unstructured interview.

The interview took place on Thursday the 16th of February, 2006 and lasted for approximately one hour, ten minutes. The exploration of the archive began with us on opposite sides of the dining table but sharing of the photographs soon compelled us to sit side-by-side with the photographs being reviewed in front of us. This may well be a physical manifestation of Collier and Collier's (1986) proposal that a triangular relationship develops between the researchers, the research and the photograph. The interview was tape-recorded and a number of photographs were taken of matters considered of significance. Field notes were taken during the interview; particularly paying attention to the requirements of effective note taking and data recording, as identified by Hammersley (1983); although the volume of data generated was so great that an accurate record was difficult to achieve and only specific events could be noted without disturbing the flow of the interview.

During the interview, a series of loose photographs were viewed and discussed. They were of grandparents, great grandparents and great great-grandparents, typically from the Victorian and Edwardian period (Appendix I). They were commercially produced, composed and formerly staged, in studio settings. The photographs were displayed in a number of ways; some un-mounted, others mounted but none were in albums, although one was framed. This was a photograph of Jillian's great great-grandparents; although small, it had a distinctive ornate wooden frame; it was black and white and not sepia; and by its presentation may be seen as transformed from the everyday, the profane, to the sacred (Durkheim, 1968, Weber, 1958). The majority of these prints were in sepia-tones, although the early photograph of the great grandparents was clear black-and-white. The production of sepia prints was not by a technical necessity, but was the fashionable form to have photographs produced in (Burgin, 2003).

The remainder of the photographs viewed were contained in four albums; three of which were solely produced by her mother; two thirds of the fourth album were produced by her father and the last third of this was by her mother. The albums generally contained photographs of the domestic as opposed to the public (Hall, 2003, Wahrman, 1995) with photographs of friends and family groups. There was particular focus on children and the events surrounding their lives, in addition to major family social events, such as weddings, thus creating a highly gendcrcd record. A major theme

running through all of the albums were photographs of holidays. During the interview this was noted when Jillian pointed out that, as her father was a teacher and had long extended holidays, they always took at least two holidays a year. Her parent's holidays from the late 1920s were an important part of both their and her life and identity. The viewing of the photographs ended at Jillian's first holiday after she had left home to train as a nurse. The interview came to an end at this stage but also seemed to be the point at which Jillian's construction of personal and social identity changed from her identity being totally taken from her family, to being taken from both her family background and her work.

My initial reaction was one of horror to the volume of data gathered. Chiozzi, (cited in Banks, 2005), states that when he began to use photographs he was 'overwhelmed with information' (p 89). It follows that the analysis of the data could only proceed if it was efficiently organized and in a readily available form that could be cross-referenced (Hammersely, 1983). To fulfil this requirement, the handwritten notes were word processed and the recording was downloaded onto the hard drive of a PC; as were the photographic images, securing the data in a safe and easily accessible archive as emphasized by Hammersley (1983). The interview was listened to twice. On the first listening, significant points of interest, or in Silverman's (2005) terms, the different types of 'puzzles' (p 166), were identified that could 'kick start' the transcription process. Finally, three short extracts were identified as 'puzzles' and were transcribed in detail. This process identified many areas of sociological interest, although three areas were the most outstanding; Jillian's identity; the relationship it has with the social class and standing of her family and the gendered construction and content of the archive. The first and second areas are identified by Harper (2002), as two of four major categories that have been investigated through photo-elicitation methods; see for example Harper, (2001), Schwartz, (1992) and Chiozzi, (1989). Although it is not possible to deal with all of these areas in this assignment, a transcribed record was kept.

The narrative of Jillian's life and identity that was constructed in this investigation was permeated by the character of Jillian's maternal grandmother. The social norms of Jillian's life and identity seem to have been set by this woman. My attention was drawn to this by the tone of the conversation when Jillian was speaking of her grandfather's business, a pawnbrokers and jewellers.

The following is part of the detailed transcription that refers to this area of interest, such a long section of the transcription is required, as the tone of the interview is as important as the information supplied. The tone of this conversation first drew attention to the underlying issues involved.

Section: Pawnbroker

After viewing a number of photographs that appeared to be of relatively affluent Victorian and Edwardian ancestors, I asked the question:

Interviewer: with hesitation.

'From what sort of background, I suppose, I mean social group or class. Where do you place your family?'

Edited:

A number of responses followed before this very crucial section.

Jillian:

After a very long hesitation, a long 'eeer' and a silence:

'My Mother worked for her father mmmm in a shop.'

Interviewer:

'What sort of shop?'

Jillian:

'Pawnbroker and jewellers.'

Long silence.

Edited:

There followed general conversation.

Interviewer:

Being not sure where to go with the line of inquiry I ask:

'And who is this?'

Jillian:

'That's aunty Marion she was my grandfather's on my mother's side sister'.

Interviewer:

'When you said pawnbroker you seemed to hesitate?'

Jillian: in a questioning, very quiet voice.

'Did I?'

Interviewer:

In a very quiet voice.

'Yeah.'

Jillian:

'Right.'

Interviewer:

'You said pawnbroker and jeweller.'

Jillian:

'Jeweller. Yeah yeah.'

She was very quiet for a few moments.

Interviewer:

'Am I reading meaning into that?'

Jillian:

'Urmm no, probably not really I think there was always a bit of, not a stigma, erm, the fact he was a pawnbroker was a..........'

The conversation trailed off.

Interviewer:

At this stage, I was feeling a little uncomfortable and decided to take a photograph.

The photographs of her grandparents being viewed at this time obviously generated considerable tension around a difficult area, being later reinforced by further comments to the undertones of class shown by her parents delayed marriage, a move to the West Midlands for work and inheritance of family wealth left to those considered more socially acceptable.

The discoveries from this photo elicitation can be clearly divided into two; the process itself and the sociological knowledge that is generated by such interviews. The greatest problems of the process itself are the amount of data that is generated, identifying the relevance of this data and its analysis. Silverman (2005) recommended that, for transcription purposes, the focus should be not on the whole interview, but on specific areas which raise the question of 'why', proposing that, through careful analysis, an overview of the general picture will follow. In this interview, it was the hesitations on the interviewee's part, which drew attention to an area that was of sociological importance, i.e. class. This information was not initially offered and it is likely that it only surfaced because of the form of the photo-elicitation and the further discussion and probing that this form of interview permits.

The elicitation was reflexive for both the interviewer and the interviewee as the process gave opportunity for reflection on the memories stimulated by the photographs; these reflections are well displayed in the transcription shown earlier. Jillian displayed hesitation and uncertainty when talking of her grandfather's business as a pawnbroker and I also shared in this hesitation and uncertainty in how to proceed with the discussion. Class and status were obviously sensitive issues within her family and significant to her own personal and social identity, issues which I also have personal concerns about.

The Archive in its storage box.

Jillian's early family photographs.

Album (No 4) the page composed by Jillian's Mother.
Showing gendered content and layout.

Album (No 4) the page composed by Jillian's Mother.
Showing gendered content and layout.

Album (No 4) the page composed by Jillian's Father.
Showing gendered content and layout.

Album (No 4) the page composed by Jillian's Father.
Showing gendered content and layout.

Bibliography

Banks, M. (2005) *Visual Methods in Social Research,* London: Sage.

Berger, J. & Mohr, J. (1967) *A Fortunate Man*, Cambridge: Granta Books.

Burgin, V. (2003) 'Looking at Photographs', in L.Wells. (Ed.) *The Photographic Reader*, London: Routledge.

Chalfen, R. (1998) 'Interpreting Family Photographs as Pictorial Communications', In J. Prosser. (Ed.) *Imaged Based Research*, London: Routledge. pp: 214-234.

Chaplin, E. (1994) *Sociology and Visual Representation*, Abingdon: Routledge.

Cliffor, J. & Marcus, G. E. (1986) *Writing Culture: The Poetic And Politics of Ethnography,* Berkeley, University of California Press.

Hall, C. (1992) *White Male and Middle Class: Explorations in Feminist History*, Cambridge: Polity Press.

Hammersley, M. & Atkinson, P. (2005) *Ethnography,* London: Routledge.

Harper, D. (2002) 'Talking about pictures: a case for photo elicitation', *Visual Studies,* Vol. 17:1.

Harper, D. (2001) *Changing Works: Visions of Lost Agriculture*, Chicago: University of Chicago Press.

Harper, D. (1998) 'An Argument for Visual Sociology', In J. Prosser (Ed.), *Image-Based Research: A sourcebook for qualitative researchers*, London: Falmer Press.

Hawkesworth, E. (1998) 'Knowers, Knowing, Known: Feminist Theories and Claims of Truth', *Signs*, Vol. 14: 3, pp: 533-557.

Holliday, R. (2004) 'Reflecting the Self', in Knowles, C. & Sweetman, P. (Eds.) *Picturing the Social Landscape: Visual Methods and the Sociological Imagination*, London: Routledge.

Knowels, C. & Sweetman, P. (Eds.) (2004) *Picturing the Social Landscape: Visual Methods and the Sociological Imagination,* London: Routledge.

Lawson, H. (1985) *Reflexivity,* London: Hutchinson.

Mills, W. C. (2000) *Sociological Imagination*, Oxford: University Press.

Pink, S. (2005) *Doing Visual Ethnography*, London: Sage.

Rose, G. (2001) *Visual Methodologies*, London: Sage Publications.

Sanders, A. (1977) *August Sanders*, London: Gordon Fraser.

Schwartz, D. (1992) *Waucoma Twilight; Generations of the Farm,* Accessed 30th January 2006. Http///sjmc.cla.umn.edu/faculy/schwartz/contents/Waucoma_Twilight/body_waucom.html

Silverman, D. (2005) *Doing Qualitative Research*, (Second Edition), London: Routledge.

Thompson. E. P. (1968) *The Making of the English Working Class,* Harmondsworth: Penguin Books.

Wahrman, D. (1995) *Imagining the Middle Class,* Cambridge: University Press.

Weber, M. (1958) *Protestant Ethic and the Spirit of Capitalism*, New York: Charles Scribner.

Part two: Reflections on Learning

Erasing the past: The destruction of a town's character

Louise Gregory

Why do we, as sociologists and as people, only start to take notice of things as they get older or become rarer or start to disappear? These two building have been standing forever in my mind and I never actually gave them much thought until this year when I started to photograph my home town for a photo-elicitation interview with my mum. It was only then that I discovered that not only were these buildings permanent fixtures in my mind, but in hers too. Now I realise that they contain years worth of shared memories and are significant in defining the town's character and landscape, not only for us but for the whole community.

The Nestlé factory, in one form or another, has stood in the same place since 1870 and now it is being demolished to provide yet another block of mass produced flats. Long gone is the factory rumoured to be the basis for Roald Dahl's 'Charlie and the Chocolate Factory', instead there will be more bland architecture in its place. Similarly, the Odeon cinema has been situated in Cambridge Street and has pleased audiences for around 70 years, until it was decided that a new and more modern version was necessary closer to the town centre. Today's cinema enthusiasts will get to visit this new cinema, but for how long? Its destruction is already impending as part of more redevelopment. Where has this left Aylesbury? With deserted and destroyed buildings and the town's character being replaced by shiny glass buildings and colourful branded shop-fronts. Architecture now seems disposable, these changes are final, with these building now near gone. In today's fast paced society it seems that there is no better time to visually record such changes, allowing them to be recognized, perhaps prevented or at least celebrated and commiserated.

In taking the photos, I finally realised the beauty of these derelict landmarks. The old cinema, a classic thirties Odeon, now unused and boarded-up (figure 1).The Nestlé factory, although perhaps less beautiful, remains significant in reminding us of the town's origins (figure 2). And what now? Now, I feel as though something ought to be done. It was not until I looked through the lens of my camera that I realised the history and memories that were being irrevocably destroyed, never to return to Aylesbury again. So, a word of warning, not just to sociologists but to everyone, appreciate what we have whilst it is still in its full glory, as once it is gone the chance to do so will be lost forever.

Figure 1: The Old Odeon Cinema, Cambridge Street, Aylesbury, 5/2/2006

Figure 2: The Nestle Factory, Tring Road, Aylesbury, 5/2/2006

A Brave New World

Lee Pinfold

Not actually having undertaken the Visual Sociology module myself, I was still eager to at least attempt some kind of visual/photographic entry for this publication. The reason for this was not because I think that I have any particular skill behind the lens, far from it – in fact these images represent my first tentative efforts in trying to come to terms with my new digital camera. Rather, it was the appeal of attempting to put some kind of visual perspective to a social phenomenon that has fascinated me for as long as I can remember.

An unusual marriage

To be sure, the social phenomena of which I speak – modern ecclesiastical architecture – has its roots in a unification of religious beliefs and secular ideals that emerged in the twentieth century. This unlikely union was based upon a shared vision of and for the future.

The establishment of the Second Vatican Council in 1962 paved the way for a Catholic renaissance worldwide, whereby it embraced a new modernising doctrine that, amongst other things, sought to converse with the modern world, rather than oppose the challenges it posed.[1] Such ideals were equally shared by the secular cultural movement, known as Modernism, which sought to encourage the re-examination of every facet of human existence – including architecture.[2] This union managed to fuse progressive Catholic beliefs with Modernist architecture. The result? An iconoclast's church.

Church of St Thomas More in Yardley, Birmingham.

An impressive Odeon-like concrete vestibule.

'An essential tenet of Modernism at the turn of the century was the need to break with the past, in order to find a national architecture or an 'architecture of our time.'[3]

A break from tradition

By the middle of the last century, post-war Britain was in the midst of transforming itself. From consensus politics, to the establishment of a progressive welfare system and major urban redevelopment and renewal, British society was certainly looking forwards towards the future. Major influences on Britain's redevelopment in the inner cities came from European Modernist architects and designers such as Alvar Aalto and Marcel Breuer. Likewise, it was within this context that modernist visionaries', and the influence they had on city planners produced the sprawling concrete jungles that came to replace the equally sprawling 'back-to-backs'.

Today however, much of this vision lies in ruins as high rise flats are being felled at an increasing rate, subways are being plugged and community shopping precincts demolished to make way for glistening new Tescos. Still, as the concrete utopia appears to be over and the urban skyline reclaimed, pockets of concrete, which have managed to stand the test of time, are starting to re-emerge as monuments to an unlikely marriage of religion and Modernism and a shared vision of a brave new world.

Note how the heavy concrete blocks are constructed to form the buttresses
and a modernist representation of a spire. Another traditional ecclesial focal
point that has undergone revision is the stained glass windows. Although not
apparent from this photograph, the depictions now take the form of rather
abstract yet equally colourful and impressive illustrations

Our Lady Help Of Christians church in Tiles Cross, Birmingham. Note
the dramatic sloping concrete crown that has replaced the traditional
church steeple. This was once green in colour.

A Pagoda styled vestibule

Abstract stained glass.

Notes

[1] The Second Vatican Council was convened by Pope John XXIII and as a gesture of its modernising intensions it invited Protestant and other Christian Orthodox organisations to witness its proceedings. The function of the Council was to combat the challenges of a modern world, and to secure a future for the Catholic Church. For more on this go to: http://mb-soft.com/believe/txs/secondvc.htm

[2] The very beginnings of the Modernist movement emerged from the Enlightenment period; a period that encapsulated the spirit of enquiry, and the questioning of religions legitimacy as the dominant source of knowledge. By the twentieth century Modernism and other associated strands such as Surrealism had become established critiques of society and its traditions. For more on this go to: http://en.wikipedia.org/wiki/Modernism

[3] Stroik, D. 'The Roots of Modernist Church Architecture' Adoremus Bulletin 3(7):1997. Also available from: http://www.adoremus.org/1097-Stroik.html (Duncan Stroik is Chair of the architecture school of Notre Dame University.)

Reflections on the practice of online participant observation: When a researcher's visuality is removed from the interaction process

Marc Bush

The Research Project

It has been claimed that online chat rooms act as social networks of support for individuals with Asperger Syndrome and function as a safe-space to interact and socialize (Singer, 1999: 65-66). I, therefore, decided to investigate, through participant observation (Brewer, 2000: 59-62), the extent to which individuals were supported by other participants in a popular and internationally represented Asperger Syndrome chat room. Moreover, I aimed to see whether this support would remain on a public chat room, with a number of live (real-time) streams of conversation (Mann & Stewart, 2000: 179). Below I have reflexively explored the epistemological, methodological and methodical limitations and possible strengths of mobilizing a virtual ethnography (Hine, 2000) in the context of this research.

Initial access was not complicated as it was tied to public (non-member) access and computer specifications (i.e. *JAVA* platform) and did not require a gatekeeper (Burgess, 1991), although it is likely that disclosure of my researcher status at the start of the research period caused a number of the potential sample to avoid a natural participation in the setting (Brewer, 2000). Despite this, I did not seem to be met with any hostility and the setting appeared to function in the same manner as it did prior to my investigation, as validated by a previous orientation visit (Mackay, 2005). A positive attribute of my role as an online researcher was that it negates somewhat a necessary power relationship within a research setting (Mann & Stewart, 2000: 169), as I could negotiate[2] between models of participant/observation (Brewer, 2000; Agar, 1980; Gold, 1958). Moreover, participants were constantly empowered and informed by instant access to information search engines[3] to research and exchange conversation topics/knowledges. Conventional problems in email-based interviewing (Kivits, 2005: 48) were overcome by allowing participants the freedom to mediate interaction (Joinson, 2005: 32). Lastly, because the interaction is *real-time* there is less of a delay and instant clarification can be sought[4] (Kivits, 2005: 43-47).

Discussion

Distinct methodological problems arose from the *public* nature of the forum and thus the extent to which I was able to gain access to the 'backstage' identities of participants (Goffman, 1963; 1990). The normal (visual) social cues used in social interaction were not present and a number of statements became open to interpretation[5] (Mann & Stewart, 2000: 162-67), therefore involuntarily empowering me with an authorial authority over the setting (Emerson et al, 1995). Furthermore, I was unable to determine the *ethnographic context* (Paccagnella cited in Orgad, 2005: 52) of interactions[6], thus meanings could be complicated further by the possibility of deceptive member profiles (Hine, 2000). As a result, due to the time restriction on the research, I was unable to create any form of internally valid data (Bryman, 2004). Therefore, even with an open-coding system and a grounded theory approach, my study was lacking in the resources to enable grounded theory-building (Glaser & Strauss, 1967). A potential solution could be the contextualizing of online interactions with offline ones, creating a sustained rapport with participants (Orgad, 2005) or mobilizing a triangulated longitudinal study (Bryman, 2004).

Finally, Sanders (2005: 71-72) notes that traditional ethical guidelines should be applied to virtual settings, therefore anonymity becomes compromised as transcripts of conversations can be stored and therefore cross-referenced (if published) to determine the individual (Hammersley & Atkinson, 1995; BSA, 2004). Furthermore, pictures of the members can be found elsewhere on the site, thus I took the approach of providing pseudonyms at the onset of the research (Rutter & Smith, 2005: 91). However Sanders (2005) later states that *participants are aware* that their conversations can be viewed in a public arena; thus the problems arise when they are not informed of the dissemination strategy, rather than during the data collection itself (Bryman, 2004).

Bibliography

Agar, M. (1980) *The Professional Stranger: An informal introduction to ethnography*, New York: Academic Press.

Brewer, J. D. (2000) *Ethnography*, Buckingham: Open University Press.

Bryman, A. (2004) *Social Research Methods* (2nd Edition), Oxford: Oxford University Press.

BSA (British Sociological Association) (2004) *Statement of Ethical Practice*,
http://www.britsoc.co.uk/new_site/user_doc/Statement%20of%20Ethical%20Practice.pdf.

Burgess, R. G. (1991) *In the Field: An introduction to field research*, London: Routledge.

Emerson, R. M., Fretz, R. I. & Shaw, L. L. (1995) *Writing Ethnographic Fieldnotes*, London: The University of Chicago Press.

Glaser, B. G. & Strauss, A. L. (1967) *The Discovery of Grounded Theory: strategies for qualitative research*, New York: Aldine de Gruyter.

Goffman, E. (1963) *Behaviour in Public Places: Notes on the social organization of gatherings*, New York: Free Press.

Goffman, E. (1990) *The Presentation of self in everyday life*, London: Penguin.

Gold, R. L. (1958) 'Roles in sociological Fieldwork' *Social Forces* 36 pp: 217-223.

Hammersley, M. & Atkinson, P. (1995) *Ethnography: Principles in practice*, London: Routledge.

Hine, C. (2000) *Virtual Ethnography*, London: Sage.

Hughes, C. (1994) 'From Field Notes to Dissertation: Analysing the stepfamily' in Bryman, A. & Burgess, R (Eds.) *Analysing Qualitative Data*, London: Routledge.

Joinson, A. H. (2005) 'Internet Behaviour and the Design of Virtual Methods' in Hine, C. (Ed.) *Virtual Methods: Issues in social research on the internet*, Oxford: Berg Press.

Kivits, J. (2005) 'Online Interviewing and the Research Relationship' in Hine, C. (Ed.) *Virtual Methods: Issues in social research on the internet*, Oxford: Berg Press.

Mackay, H. (2005) 'New Connections, Familiar Settings: issues in the ethnographic study of new media use at home' in Hine, C. (Ed.) *Virtual*

Methods: Issues in social research on the internet, Oxford: Berg Press.

Mann, C. & Stewart, F. (2000) *Internet Communication and Qualitative Research: a handbook for researching online*, London: Sage.

Odih, P. (2004) 'Using the Internet' in Seale, C. (Ed.) *Researching Society and Culture* (2nd Edition), London: Sage.

Orgad, S. (2005) 'From Online to Offline and Back: moving from Online to Offline relationships with research informants' in Hine, C. (Ed.) *Virtual Methods: Issues in social research on the internet*, Oxford: Berg Press.

Rutter, J. & Smith, G. W. H. (2005) 'Ethnographic Presence in a Nebulous Setting' in Hine, C. (Ed.) *Virtual Methods: Issues in social research on the internet*, Oxford: Berg Press.

Sanders, T. (2005) 'Researching the Online Sex Work Community' in Hine, C. (Ed.) *Virtual Methods: Issues in social research on the internet*, Oxford: Berg Press.

Schatzman, L. & Strauss, A. L. (1973) *Field Research: Strategies for a natural sociology*, New Jersey: Prentice-Hall.

Singer, J. (1999) "Why Can't You be Normal for Once in Your Life?': From a 'problem with no name' to the emergence of a new category of difference' in Corker, M. & French, S. (Eds.) *Disability Discourse*, Buckingham: Open University Press.

Appendix A

The following extracts are from my research report, based on the recording
strategy of participation, as suggested by Schatzman & Strauss (1973)

Observational Notes

The specific context related to his 'extreme boredom' of superficial
interactions and a want for deeper debates on which he was interested;
socialism and peace movements being the case in point. The conversation
was based around *Joey*'s weighing up of whether or not to join a local
debating society at his university in a European country.

Joey is overly critical of his ability to find similar minded individuals. This
sense of alienation from 'normal' conversation is continually reaffirmed
through a wholly defeatist attitude, even when faced with constant network
support of the two main actors on the site. The main two supporters
consistently left a pause in typing then wrote longer paragraphs to clarify
their opposition to *Joey*'s defeatist attitude. This was contrasted by *Joey*'s
own, short, despondent comments. Furthermore, whereas *Joey* used
emoticons (digital emotion icons) to emphasise his statements, the two main
supporters did not draw on pictorial (emoticon) use. It is important to note
that additional supporters on the chat room were temporarily engaged with
the main topic of conversation by adding comments of 'how'd u mean?!?'
and :^((a 'sad face' emoticon), before returning to the alternative topic of
conversation (which at the time was based on a parody of Douglas Adams'
The Hitchhiker's Guide to the Galaxy: A trilogy in five parts.)

Theoretical Notes

I regard the support of the main two protagonists to be based on their prior
experience of interacting and dealing with *Joey*'s insecurities. Their
comments seem to allude to previous examples of his self-fatalism and his
need for constant reassurance. Moreover, the intermittent support offered by
other protagonists in the chat room and the over use of emoticons suggests
that *Joey*'s fatalism is a continuous presence in the chat room. This can be
verified by exploring the members' only forums where *Joey* discusses
similar issues, based around specific themes, including *love and romance*
and *friends*.

Analytic Memos

Goffman (1963: 33-79) notes that the management of 'side/subordinate involvements' is key to successful social interaction. Thus one can assume, as suggested by Goffman, that the level of investment in a main involvement and management of side/subordinate/auto involvements will affect the level or empathetic support offered by others in a public arena. Interestingly, in this particular setting, the over-vocalized management of side intentions[7] does not perturb individuals from the conversation and on many instances they become the main topic of conversation, thus possibly challenging Goffman's core theory in the context of a virtual public space. Intermittently, participants would mention a side-involved, for instance the sort of pasta they were eating, which would spark an elaborate, extremely factual dialogue from the previously dormant participants about the pasta's genealogy, political context, nutritional constitution and so forth.

Methodological Field Notes

It has occurred to me that this form of participant observation has a scopophillic element to it, in that I am attempting to interact in the chat room through encouraging interaction, however with a need to avoid interrupting the timing and sequencing of the interaction. Unfortunately, when I felt that I had remained dormant too long and become somewhat a detected observer, I interjected in the sequencing of the conversation with a side comment in support of *Joey*, however because it interrupted a movement in the conversation (something I failed to see as I was typing at the time), my message was misconstrued and confused and explanation was demanded (i.e. 'what?' and 'were you talking to me?') thus altering the focus of attention onto myself. A second contributing factor to the confusion of my statement was my temporary *perceived* disengagement from the conversation at hand (See Sanders, 2005: 75).

---

[1] See Hughes (1994) for an informed discussion of the negotiation between models of participant observation
[2] i.e. *Google* (http://www.google.co.uk/) or *Wikipedia* (http://en.wikipedia.org/wiki/Main_Page)
[3] For an example of technical problems of sequencing and timing on the internet see **Methodological Notes** in **Appendix A**
[4] Especially in the use of emoticons (Kivits, 2005: 40)
[5] Both *online* and *offline* contexts (Odih, 2004: 287)
[6] An external vocalization through narration of current side or subordinated involvement; for example '[Name] is eating salted chips and [Name] is happy' or 'this light is drivin' me crazy'.

The Hedgecarpenter

Steve Birks

'Hedgecarpenter'.
Warwickshire, November 2005.

This image was acquired on a November afternoon in 2006 as part of a visual sociology undergraduate project inquiring into identity. The study focused on the expression of personal and social identity through the clothing worn in cold working conditions. Photographs were taken on building sites, in public gardens and butcher's shops.

This photograph of Ralph was taken at the side of the Fosse Way near Halford in Warwickshire. I noticed him working at the side of the road, on impulse stopped, turned my car around and introduced myself and my project to him. In a very free flowing conversation, that lasted forty minutes, we discovered that we had shared knowledge of the area and the type of work in which he was involved. Three photographs were taken without on my part a great deal of thought as to the lighting or composition.

Afterwards, I continued on my journey and for the first time in field research, felt a compelling need to immediately write notes, as opposed to note writing being a chore.

Six months later, I have completed my visual sociology module and have time to reflect on the use of visual methods in sociology and what I have discovered from taking this image.

The most important discovery I have made was a non scientific one, if you have a 'gut' reaction, regardless of the constraints placed on you by your research, act on the impulse, change direction, let your imagination flow. The urge to write notes was the indication that I had something of interest, unfortunately however, my reaction was a concern with writing good field notes rather than reacting to the immediate situation and following the puzzle. I needed to hear others comment that I had an interesting image before I became aware that I had a 'special' photograph. If I had followed my initial reactions, I would have adopted a different approach to the analysis of the image and possibly a more valuable one.